I. Background and Introduction

The merger proposed by the Union Pacific Railroad Co. (UP) and the Southern Pacific Transportation Co. (SP) in 1995 would have combined two of the three largest railroads in the West and created the largest railroad in the country. According to Kwoka and White,[2] the combined railroad would have 35,000 miles of track and $9.5 billion in revenues. UP urged the Interstate Commerce Commission (ICC) – which became the Surface Transportation Board (hereafter STB or Board) in 1996 – to approve the merger, claiming that it would generate substantial cost reductions and service improvements and thereby strengthen rail competition in the West. UP viewed the merger as an opportunity to rehabilitate SP, which UP and many others considered an ailing firm with diminishing competitive effectiveness. Many SP shippers supported the merger.

The Department of Justice (DOJ), by contrast, contended that the two rail networks contained extensive stretches of parallel track, including the lines from south Texas through Houston to Memphis, St. Louis, and Chicago; the lines from Houston to New Orleans and San Antonio; and the Central Corridor.[3] According to Kwoka and White, the combination of the two railroads would reduce to two ("3-to-2 traffic") or sometimes one ("2-to-1 traffic") the number of railroads serving hundreds, and perhaps thousands, of shippers throughout the West. DOJ took the position that the merger proposal would result in "overwhelming competitive harm" in a large number of markets as the combined railroad exercised market power unilaterally or in the form of coordinated behavior with other carriers. Other merger protestants included shippers and shipper organizations, and various railroads. The STB also received submissions from other federal agencies, including the U.S. Department of Transportation (DOT), and from state and local agencies, and labor organizations. Merger opponents considered the proposed remedy to competitive problems – involving trackage rights[4] – to be inadequate. They recommended

---

[2]John E. Kwoka, Jr. and Lawrence J. White, "Manifest Destiny? The Union Pacific and Southern Pacific Railroad Merger (1996)," in *The Antitrust Revolution: Economics, Competition, and Policy*, edited by John E. Kwoka, Jr. and Lawrence J. White, (New York: Oxford University Press, 2004), 27-51. See also Lawrence J. White, "Staples-Office Depot and UP-SP: An Antitrust Tale of Two Proposed Mergers," in *Measuring Market Power,* 153-174, edited by Daniel J. Slottje. *Contributions to Economic Analysis*, Vol. 255 (Amsterdam: Elsevier Science, North-Holland, 2002). Kwoka and White participated in the ICC/STB merger proceeding, filing comments on behalf of merger protestants Dow Chemical Company and the Kansas City Southern Railway Company, respectively.

[3]The Central Corridor was described as an area running from St. Louis to Oakland via Denver, Salt Lake City, and Reno. Department of Justice, Brief Before the Surface Transportation Board (June 3, 1996), DOJ-14 in *Union Pacific Corp. – Control & Merger – Southern Pacific Corp.*, STB Finance Docket 32760, at 2.

[4]These are rights that one railroad (tenant) secures from another railroad (landlord) to move freight over the landlord's lines using the tenant's own locomotives, cars, and crews. The

instead either rejection of the merger application or else conditioning its approval on the full divestiture of rail lines to other railroads where competition was threatened. DOJ and others, as reported in Kwoka and White (2004), and White (2002), also considered many of the efficiencies claimed for the merger to be overstated, or not recognizable as public benefits, or else achievable through alternative means. Kwoka and White also note that certain parties took issue with claims of SP's deteriorating financial condition and competitive effectiveness.

UP acknowledged the horizontal overlaps between it and SP and sought to resolve competitive concerns regarding 2-to-1 shippers by entering into an extensive trackage rights agreement with the Burlington Northern and Santa Fe Railway (BNSF), the other large railroad in the West. This involved almost 4,000 miles of track (including the 2,100 Denver-to-Oakland segment of the Central Corridor). UP also agreed to divest another few hundred miles of track to BNSF. Merger applicants did not propose a fix for 3-to-2 shippers, contending for various reasons that coordinated or cooperative behavior even with as few as two railroads would be difficult.

In its decision of August 6, 1996,[5] the STB concluded that on balance the proposed merger would be in the public interest.[6] The Board found the BNSF trackage rights fix for 2-to-1 traffic to be adequate and that there would be important service improvements and efficiencies flowing from the merger. A major benefit of the merger, according to the Board, was that it would permit the financially weak SP to become part of a large, financially healthy rail system and thereby be in a position to sustain efficient operations and maintain a viable level of investment in its plant. A revitalized UP/SP in turn would be better positioned to compete with the newly merged, more efficient BNSF, to the benefit of shippers in the West. The STB's assessment of competitive issues, efficiency claims, and SP's financial condition is generally

---

tenant pays a per car and mileage fee to the landlord. As a merger remedy, these rights are imposed by the STB in an effort to restore competition where it otherwise would be threatened by the merger.

[5]Surface Transportation Board, *Union Pacific/Southern Pacific Merger*, 1 S.T.B. 233 (1996).

[6]Unlike antitrust agencies, the STB must formally approve mergers and in so doing uses a public interest standard that involves a broader balancing of public benefits (service improvements and efficiencies) with any competitive harm. White (2002), at 163-164, contends that the ICC/STB historically has been more inclined than the antitrust agencies to accept efficiency claims, and that there has been a strong tendency for the ICC/STB to approve rail merger applications. Likewise, Massa has noted the tendency for the ICC and STB to approve rail merger applications. See Salvatore Massa, "Are All Railroad Mergers in the Public Interest? An Analysis of the Union Pacific Merger with Southern Pacific," *Transportation Law Journal* 24 (Spring-Summer 1997), at 415.

accepted in a financial analysis retrospective of the merger.[7]

The Board thought that the proposed alternative remedy – rail-line divestitures – would be overreaching and would impose a greater burden than monitoring the trackage rights agreement. Regarding 3-to-2 traffic in particular, the STB concluded that not taking action here was consistent with its previous rail merger decisions, which were based on the Board's experience that two railroads were sufficient to provide competition. The Board did announce, as a further condition for merger approval, oversight for five years to determine whether the conditions it imposed had effectively addressed the competitive problems they were intended to remedy.

This paper has two main purposes. One is to evaluate the efficiencies prospectively claimed for this merger against the relevant regulatory/antitrust standards and economic principles. The second purpose is to assess, to the extent permitted by available evidence, whether the claimed merger efficiencies were realized. As a retrospective case study, the UP/SP merger provides an unusual opportunity to examine this aspect of merger analysis because it provides post-merger evidence on actual efficiency outcomes as well as detailed information on efficiency claims. It is also an opportunity because there is significant overlap between regulatory and antitrust standards for the treatment of those claims, particularly regarding the extent to which such efficiencies are considered to be specific to the merger. The efficiency analysis undertaken here may be especially useful for merger enforcement policy because of the skepticism that exists about merger-related efficiency claims and their realization.[8]

The paper does not examine the nature and extent of any anticompetitive effects associated with the UP/SP merger. Therefore, it does not attempt to compare merger benefits with merger costs as part of an overall welfare analysis, although it does consider whether post-merger rate trends are consistent with efficiencies being realized. Section II organizes and describes the merger benefits claimed in the merger application. Section III examines the STB's review of the claimed benefits, including its consideration of arguments made by the merger's opponents, and assesses the magnitude of the claimed efficiencies and whether they are public rather than private in nature, fairly attributable to the merger, not reasonably achievable through other means less likely to raise competitive concerns, and verifiable. All information cited in Sections II and III was obtained from public sources. Section IV reviews available evidence from public and certain normally non-public sources to determine whether the merger efficiencies were actually realized to the extent and in the form claimed.

---

[7]Michael Conant, "Union Pacific Merger of Southern Pacific," in *Railroad Bankruptcies and Mergers from Chicago West: 1975-2001: Financial Analysis and Regulatory Critique. Research in Transportation Economics*, Vol. 7 (Amsterdam: Elsevier JAI, 2004), at 117-133.

[8]See, for example, Craig W. Conrath and Nicholas A. Widnell, "Efficiency Claims in Merger Analysis: Hostility or Humility?" *George Mason Law Review* 7 (1999), 685-705.

II. Merger Benefits Claimed in Merger Application

A. Potential for Merger Benefits

The maps on the next two pages show how the UP and SP route networks would fit together as a result of the proposed merger. The two route networks generally were in the same geographic region and therefore overlapped to a significant extent, with many parallel route segments (e.g., Oakland-Denver, Houston-New Orleans, San-Antonio-Chicago). These horizontal overlaps and the many common service points suggested the possibility of duplicative facilities, and created a potential for cost savings and service improvements through consolidation and integration.[9] In addition, the two route networks were complementary in nature, with UP filling gaps in SP's system (e.g., between the Pacific Northwest and the Midwest) and SP filling gaps in UP's system (e.g., between TX and CA). This created the potential for improved routings (e.g., combining segments of each railroad to create more direct routes) and single-line service[10] to more points in the West, both of which appeal to shippers.

The merger benefits, highlighted by UP and SP in their merger application to the ICC, included both quantified and unquantified elements. Both were supported by verified statements from in-house officials and outside consultants. As discussed below, quantified benefits included – in declining order of importance – merger efficiencies and cost savings (total operating benefits), shipper logistics savings, and net revenue (traffic) gains. Unquantified

---

[9]Grimm and Plaistow characterize the UP/SP merger as having "unprecedented parallel effects," in contrast to the largely end-to-end rail mergers from the early 1980s up to the mid-1990s. End-to-end rail mergers refer to combinations of railroads with route networks that are largely in different geographic regions but are connected at the points they do have in common. See Curtis M. Grimm and Joseph J. Plaistow, "Competitive Effects of Railroad Mergers," *Transportation Research Forum* 38 (1999), 65-78. Similarly, the General Accounting Office (GAO) characterizes the UP/SP merger as having "significant parallel components," as compared to other rail mergers during the second half of the 1990s, which it characterizes as "largely end-to-end." The latter include Burlington Northern/Santa Fe (1995), CSX/Norfolk Southern/Conrail (1998), and Canadian National/Illinois Central (1999). See General Accounting Office, *Freight Railroad Regulation: Surface Transportation Board's Oversight Could Benefit From Evidence Better Identifying How Mergers Affect Rates*. GAO-01-689 (July 2001), at 30-32.

[10]Single-line service means that a shipper's freight moves from origin to destination over the tracks of one railroad, thereby avoiding the cost and delay associated with interchange of freight cars between railroads.

SP Fills Gaps in the UP System

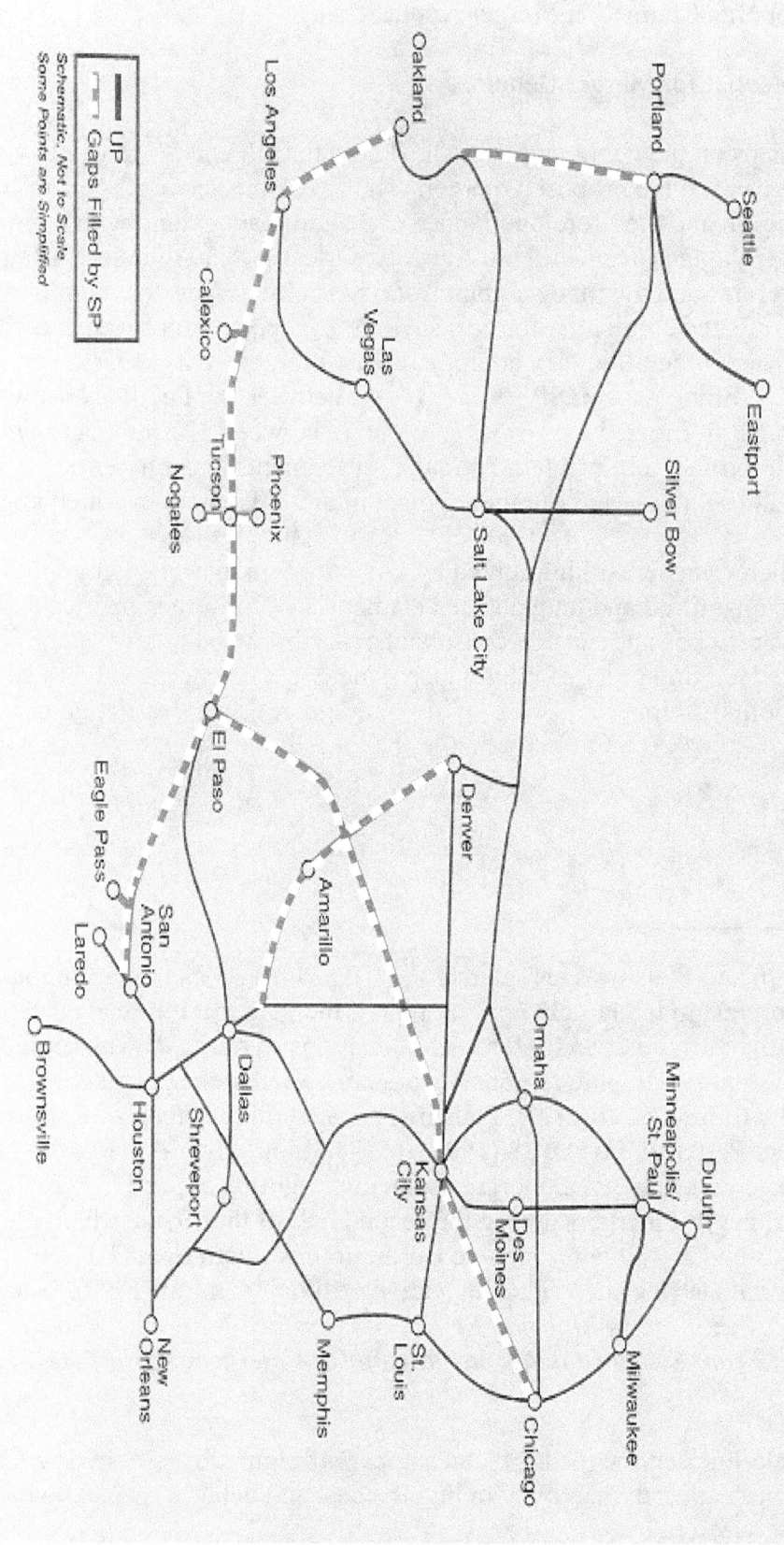

Legend:
- —— UP
- ▦▦ Gaps Filled by SP

Schematic, Not to Scale
Some Points are Simplified

Source: UP/SP-24, "Railroad Merger Application" (November 30, 1995), Vol. 3, diagram at 10, in *Union Pacific Corp. - Control & Merger -Southern Pacific Corp.*, STB Finance Docket 32760.

UP Fills Gaps in the SP System

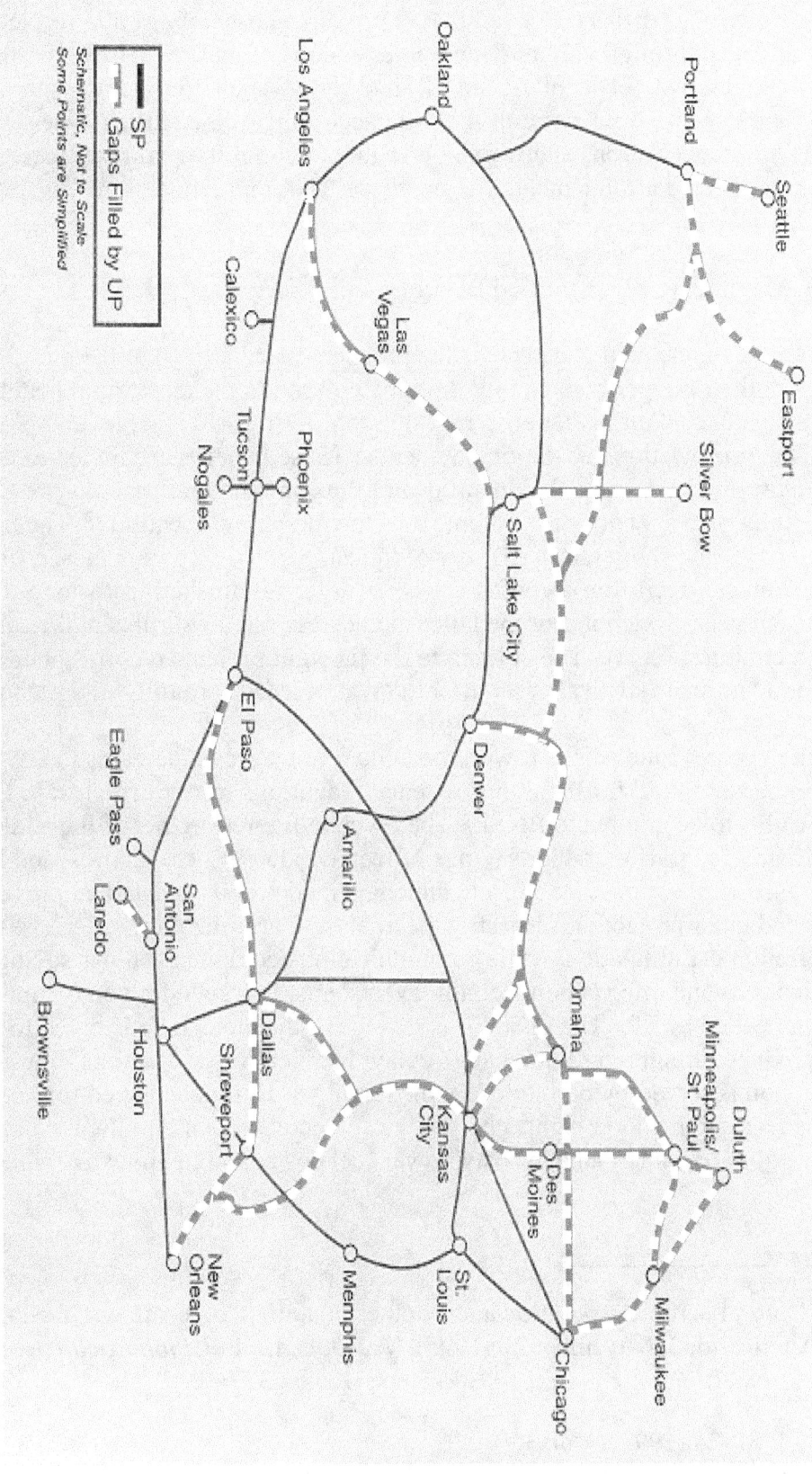

Source: UP/SP-24, "Railroad Merger Application" (November 30, 1995), Vol. 3, diagram at 11, in *Union Pacific Corp. - Control & Merger -Southern Pacific Corp.*, STB Finance Docket 32760.

benefits included expanded single-line service, more efficient routings (e.g., shorter routes, directional operation), and increased capacity and capital investment.

The merging parties conceded that in principle cost savings and service improvements could be achieved through voluntary agreements short of merger. However, they argued that history (including that between UP and SP) had shown such arrangements to be inefficient. Voluntary agreements were difficult to reach, according to the parties, where two railroads did not have similar motivations and were not willing to commit equal resources. Even if agreed to, moreover, negotiated arrangements frequently proved impractical in reality.[11]

B. Magnitudes of Quantified Benefits

Table 1 on the next page shows the prospective benefits that the merging railroads quantified in their merger application. For any column in the table, total benefits are the sum of net revenue gains, operating benefits, and shipper logistics savings, less employee relocation costs and labor protection/separation payments. These benefits are linked to the steps to be taken to consolidate and coordinate the operations of the combined railroad, as presented in the 400 page operating plan appearing in Volume 3 of the merger application.[12] The benefits, and associated costs, are shown for each year of the anticipated five-year merger-implementation period. "Annual" (recurring) benefits and costs are distinguished from "one-time" benefits and costs for each year. Examples of the latter include the sale of surplus real estate (benefit) and capital expenditures (cost). The column to the far right projects recurring benefits of $750.6 million for a "normal" (typical) year after the two railroads are fully integrated.

The "net revenue gains" row in the table refers to revenue gains to UP/SP from merger-induced increases in rail traffic, minus revenue reductions from traffic lost to BNSF due to the trackage rights to be granted to BNSF. The revenue figures are net of the additional cost of handling increased traffic. Labor savings reflect avoided wages, salaries, and benefits, although, as shown further down in the table, adjustment is made for associated employee relocation expenses and labor protection/separation payments. Car utilization reflects savings from more efficient freight car utilization, while communications/computers shows savings from combining communications and information technology systems, less spending on computer and related equipment needed by SP. The operations savings in the table are attributed to more efficient routings; reduced freight-car interchange delay; heavier bridge loadings; line abandonments; savings at points served by both (closure of freight yards, reduced need for vehicles, elimination of various fees and trackage rights charges, etc.); decreased car and track maintenance costs; better control of loss and damage costs; lower fuel costs; and net trackage rights proceeds ($47.2

---

[11]Union Pacific Corporation and Southern Pacific Corporation, UP/SP-24, "Railroad Merger Application" (November 30, 1995), Vol. 3, at 12, in *Union Pacific Corp. - Control & Merger - Southern Pacific Corp.*, STB Finance Docket 32760.

[12]UP/SP-24 (1995), Vol. 3.

Table 1

Summary of Prospective Benefits
UP/SP Merger
Five-Year Implementation Plan
($ in Thousands)

	Year 1 Annual	Year 1 One-Time	Year 2 Annual	Year 2 One-Time	Year 3 Annual	Year 3 One-Time	Year 4 Annual	Year 4 One-Time	Year 5 Annual	Year 5 One-Time	Normal Year
Net Revenue Gains	$22,814		$53,232		$60,836		$68,441		$76,045		$76,045
Labor Savings	90,585		222,973		255,194		258,390		261,150		261,150
Non-Labor Savings											
Car Utilization	3,803		8,874		10,142		11,409		12,677		12,677
Communications/ Computers	(11,861)	(82,479)	821	(27,716)	26,997	(2,960)	21,719	(1,223)	14,214		14,214
Operations	46,501	(529,947)	102,822	(394,951)	130,467	(266,539)	144,122	(124,960)	157,756	9,905	157,756
General/ Administrative	110,797	(139,805)	116,070	35,300	125,245	62,300	137,970		137,970		137,970
Total Operating Benefits	239,825	(472,621)	451,560	(387,367)	548,045	(207,199)	573,611	(126,183)	583,767	9,905	583,767
Labor Protection/ Separation		(107,411)		(67,251)		(11,926)		(1,726)			
Employee Relocation		(26,594)		(44,742)		(3,914)					
Shipper Logistics Savings	27,251		63,585		72,669		81,752		90,836		90,836
Total Benefits	$289,890	(606,626)	568,377	(499,360)	681,549	(223,039)	723,804	(127,910)	750,648	9,905	750,648

Source: UP/SP-22, "Railroad Merger Application" (November 30, 1995), Vol. 1, table at 93, in *Union Pacific Corp. - Control & Merger - Southern Pacific Corp.*, STB Finance Docket 32760.

million) to UP/SP from BNSF.[13] The general/administrative category refers to savings from combining the management and administrative functions of the two railroads. Examples include combining central office functions in fewer buildings, and reduced supply and procurement costs. Thus, the predicted cost savings include reductions in fixed (overhead) as well as variable costs.

The "shipper logistics savings" shown in the table are the sum of (1) cost savings to shippers as a result of projected traffic diversions of truckload shipments to UP/SP intermodal (truck/rail) service, due to merger-related service improvements in several traffic corridors, and (2) cost savings to shippers previously using SP for rail carload traffic between selected points in the West, due to savings in time and mileage brought about by the merger.

The merger applicants recognized that operating efficiencies and traffic gains could be realized only by making substantial investments to upgrade and increase the capacity of several SP lines and yards, improving certain UP lines, connecting the railroads' tracks, constructing new intermodal facilities, and improving SP's technological capabilities. UP committed to making these investments in its merger application and operating plan. Many of those projects would be completed during the first year but others were expected to take two years or more. The table was constructed under the assumption that 40% of the required capital expenditures would be made during the first year of combined operation, 30% during the second year, 20% during the third year, and 10% during the fourth year.[14] These up-front capital expenditures meant that one-time costs would be incurred early on and that ongoing benefits from traffic gains and operating efficiencies would start out relatively small, as the table shows, and then increase during the five-year period.

C. Enumeration of Unquantified Benefits

1. Expanded Single-Line Service and Improved Routings

Unquantified benefits featured by merger applicants included service improvements in the form of expanded single-line service and more efficient routes. The generally recognized benefits of single-line service include elimination of freight car interchanges and associated costs and delays, simplification of rate negotiations, and reduced billing errors. These in turn yield better service and allow shippers to expand markets geographically. Two of the numerous

---

[13]Verified statement of Mark J. Draper and Dale W. Salzman, in Union Pacific Corporation and Southern Pacific Corporation, UP/SP-22, "Railroad Merger Application" (November 30, 1995), Vol. 1, at 368, in *Union Pacific Corp. - Control & Merger - Southern Pacific Corp.*, STB Finance Docket 32760.

[14]Draper and Salzman, UP/SP-22 (1995), Vol. 1, at 364.

examples of expanded single-line service provided by merger applicants, and noted by the STB[15] are as follows:

> UP/SP merger will offer a new single-line service between many UP points in the Pacific Northwest (Seattle/Tacoma, Spokane, and a Canadian gateway) and many SP points in CA, AZ, NM, and west Texas, including Mexican gateways.
>
> The merger will link UP and SP route networks in TX to UP's routes from Denver to UT, ID, MT, OR, and WA, via SP's route from Ft. Worth to Denver, providing new single-line service for shipments between those regions.

UP and SP also argued that shorter, more direct routes could be assembled by combining key segments of each railroad's lines. These track-mileage reductions implied train-crew and fuel cost savings, and lower rates and faster service for freight traffic on the new routes. Numerous examples were provided in the merger application,[16] including the following:

> Los Angeles - Memphis. Merged firm will assemble segments of UP's and SP's lines via El Paso to create the shortest route. SP's route dips into southern TX while UP's route goes as far north as WY and NE. Combining routes would reduce SP's mileage between Los Angeles and Memphis by 283 miles, and reduce UP's mileage by 580 miles.
>
> Northern California - Midwest. SP has the most direct route between northern CA and Ogden, UT, while UP has the most direct routes from Ogden to the Midwest. Segments will be assembled to create a through route that is shorter than either existing route. A combined UP/SP route between Oakland and Chicago would be 388 miles shorter than SP's route and 189 miles shorter than UP's route.

Other routes could be improved, according to merger applicants, by introducing directional operation. Most of UP's lines and all of SP's lines were single track. The primary cause of train delay on single track is head-on "meets between trains," and adding trains increases meets and congestion geometrically. Using a directional system, the number of meets can decrease, and trains can run faster, without adding new track capacity. In the South Central region, for example, one line will be operated northbound to Chicago, St. Louis, and Memphis, and the parallel line will be operated southbound to San Antonio, Houston, and Dallas/Ft. Worth.

---

[15]Surface Transportation Board, 1 S.T.B. 233 (1996), at 564-565.

[16]UP/SP-22 (1995), Vol. 1, at 29.

2. Increased Capacity and Capital Investment

Also claimed by applicants as a merger benefit, but not included with the quantified benefits, was the approximately $1.3 billion that UP/SP planned to spend over four years to upgrade lines and to add new facilities so that merger-related synergies could be realized. These investments are described in the operating plan appearing in Volume 3 of the merger application. Table 2 on the next page lists many of the more significant rail corridor upgrade projects contemplated. Examples of capital expenditures planned for other facilities included $67.5 million for the construction of a new intermodal facility in the Inland Empire (eastern Los Angeles basin); $38.2 million for upgrading and rehabilitating SP's Roseville Yard (northeast of Sacramento); and $21 million to build a new running repair facility at West Colton (Inland Empire).

III. Examination of STB Review of Claimed Merger Benefits

A. STB Merger Review Standards

In reviewing rail merger proposals, the STB is required by statute to apply a public interest standard. Under that standard, it must consider the public benefits of a proposed merger and weigh them against any competitive harm in deciding whether the transaction would be in the public interest. The STB defines public benefits to be efficiency gains that take the form of cost reductions, cost savings, and service improvements.[17] Cost reductions occur if a larger rail operation enables the combined railroad to exploit economies of scale, scope, or traffic density commonly found in the rail industry.[18] Savings arise in fixed and variable costs if consolidation leads, for example, to elimination of interchanges, more efficient movements, reduced overhead,

---

[17] Surface Transportation Board, 1 S.T.B. 233 (1996), at 363

[18] Some have suggested, however, that rail mergers may create combined firms that exceed efficient scale. Kwoka and White (2004) have asserted that the UP/SP merger would create a larger organization which would be more difficult to manage and integration could lead to inefficiencies. Recently, Chapin and Schmidt undertook data envelopment analysis (DEA) to measure the efficiency of the rail industry. DEA involves application of linear programming techniques to determine production frontiers. Chapin and Schmidt find that while rail mergers (1980-1993) substantially increased technical efficiency in the operation of track networks, they decrease scale efficiencies at the firm level by even more. Their results suggest that many rail mergers result in firms that are larger than an efficient scale. See Allison Chapin and Stephen Schmidt, "Do Mergers Improve Efficiency? Evidence from Deregulated Rail Freight," *Journal of Transport Economics and Policy* 33 (1999), 147-162. By comparison, a more recent study of rail mergers (for the period 1983-1997, during which rail mergers became ever larger) generally finds significant cost reductions associated with the pure scale effects of combining railroads. See Wesley Wilson and John Bitzan, "Industry Costs and Consolidation: Efficiency Gains and Mergers in the Railroad Industry," Upper Great Plains Transportation Institute, MPC Report No. 03-145 (June 2003).

Table 2

**Proposed UP/SP
Corridor Upgrades**

Line Segment	Description of Upgrade	Capital Investment
SP Sunset Route: El Paso, TX-Los Angeles, CA	Create over 100 miles of additional double track	$221.4 million
SP Golden State Route: Topeka, KS-El Paso,TX	Install CTC; install $24.7 million of welded rail; strengthen bridges; construct or extend ten sidings	$145.8 million
UP T&P Line: Ft. Worth, TX-El Paso, TX	Install $74.3 million of welded rail and ties; extend or build 18 sidings; other track and signal work	$125.4 million
UP OKT Line: Herington,KS-Ft.Worth,TX	Install $25.3 million of welded rail; build, extend or upgrade 22 sidings; strengthen bridges	$91.5 million
UP KP Line: Denver, CO-Topeka, KS	Install $49.4 million of welded rail; build or extend 15 sidings; other track and bridge work	$86.6 million
UP Line: Iowa Jct., LA - Avondale, LA	Install $16.4 million of welded rail; strengthen bridges; build and extend sidings	$44.3 million
Joint Line: Big Sandy, TX-Ft. Worth, TX	Build or extend sidings and double track; new crossovers	$25.2 million
SP Mococo Line: Tracy, CA-Martinez, CA	Install $14.7 million of welded rail; build sidings	$21.0 million
Paired Track: Alazon, NV-Weso, NV	Signal for two-way operation; install crossovers	$20.5 million

Source: UP/SP-24, "Railroad Merger Application" (November 30, 1995), Vol. 3, table at 23, in *Union Pacific Corp. - Control & Merger - Southern Pacific Corp.*, STB Finance Docket 32760.

and elimination of duplicative facilities. The STB does not seem to require, but does expect, that these benefits will be passed on to most shippers (to an extent that varies with competitive conditions) in the form of reduced rates or improved service.[19]

The STB's consideration of both competitive harm and efficiency gains is consistent with antitrust policy[20] but involves, to a greater extent, the weighing of economic merger benefits against competitive harms. This shows itself in the STB's attention to mitigation by remedial conditions and post-merger oversight. The STB contrasts its approach with antitrust review, characterizing the latter as giving less weight to arguments that cost savings justify mergers that otherwise might be viewed as anticompetitive.[21] This suggests that the STB standard more closely resembles a total welfare standard where significant weight is given to producer as well as consumer welfare. In principle, the STB could approve a merger that antitrust authorities might challenge under a consumer welfare standard. As a practical matter, however, the STB's expectation that merger-related cost savings be passed on to shippers suggests more of a focus on consumer welfare.

The STB's "public interest" standard is broader than antitrust standards for mergers, allowing for consideration of other factors, including the impact of a merger on employees. Here too, in principle, STB approval or disapproval could diverge from antitrust authority decisions to challenge or not to challenge a merger. At the time of the UP/SP merger application, a longstanding national transportation policy affirmatively encouraged railroad mergers and consolidations that were in the public interest.[22] The public interest in this sense included rationalizing railroad infrastructure and eliminating excess capacity, which, among other things, could impart an STB bias in favor of finding public benefits.

Within this general framework, the next two subsections examine the STB's review of the nature and extent of the merger benefits (quantified and unquantified benefits, respectively) claimed by the applicants in this case, and its review of the testimony to the contrary. Because the author did not have access to all or better information than that available to the STB, the assessment presented below focuses on the STB's economic reasoning and the apparent thoroughness of its review.

B. Assessment of STB Review of Quantified Benefits

---

[19]1 S.T.B 233 (1996), at 369. This expectation appears to be based not on any formal "pass-through analysis" but rather on the STB's general experience since 1980 with rail cost reductions (through merger or otherwise) and related rate trends. 1 S.T.B. 233 (1996), at 370.

[20]As contained in Department of Justice and Federal Trade Commission, *Horizontal Merger Guidelines* (1992, revised 1997).

[21]Surface Transportation Board, 1 S.T.B. 233 (1996), at 367.

[22]Commissioner Owen, commenting, Surface Transportation Board, *Union Pacific/Southern Pacific Merger*, 1 S.T.B. 233 (1996), at 540.

During the ICC/STB's merger review proceedings, the claimed merger benefits were challenged by certain parties, most notably by DOJ and the Kansas City Southern Railway Company. Most skeptical was DOJ's economic consultant, Laurits Christensen, who, in his verified statement, argued that the quantified benefits attributed to the proposed merger were significantly overstated.[23] In the view of Christensen and DOJ, the benefits improperly included the following:

> (1) efficiencies which would occur even in the absence of the merger because of favorable productivity trends[24] in the railroad industry,

> (2) transfers from one party to another that represent private gains rather than social benefits, and

> (3) benefits that UP and SP could achieve (e.g., improved equipment utilization, more efficient routing, single-line service) through voluntary contractual arrangements (e.g., leasing, trackage rights, joint marketing) as an alternative to merger.

As pointed out in DOJ's accompanying brief, the discounting of such claimed "benefits" is

---

[23]Verified statement of Dr. Laurits R. Christensen on behalf of the U.S. Department of Justice in DOJ-8 (April 9, 1996), redacted version, at 3, in *Union Pacific Corp. - Control & Merger - Southern Pacific Corp.*, STB Finance Docket 32760.

[24]According to Christensen, the STB's productivity adjustment factor indicated that productivity growth in the rail industry averaged 5.9% annually for the 1989-1994 period leading up to the UP/SP merger proposal. Christensen also cited a study by Berndt, et al. which sought to measure the differential effects of deregulation (1980 Staggers Rail Act) and mergers on cost and productivity for the period 1974-1986. By examining shifts in estimated translog cost functions, they found that mergers during the early post-Staggers period (which were primarily end-to-end) tended to have a cost reducing impact but one of diminishing magnitude over time. Deregulation tended to have a cost reducing impact of increasing magnitude over time. By comparison, the merger-related cost reducing impact tended to be smaller and shorter lived. See Ernst R. Berndt, Ann F. Friedlaender, Judy Shaw-Er Wang Chang, and Christopher A. Vellturo, "Cost Effects of Mergers and Deregulation in the U.S. Rail Industry," *The Journal of Productivity Analysis* 4 (1993), 127-144. Such studies provide support for the negative commentary about rail mergers by Massa (1997) and others. A subsequent study, Chapin and Schmidt (1999), includes rail mergers for a longer period (1980-1993), albeit still primarily end-to-end mergers, and also attributes observed efficiency improvements more to deregulation than to mergers. By comparison, Wilson and Bitzan (2003) focus on rail mergers for the period 1983-1997, which include very large mergers (Burlington Northern/Santa Fe and CSX/Norfolk Southern/Conrail, as well as UP/SP) with some, such as UP/SP, having significant parallel components. In that study, merger-related consolidation is found to account for approximately 17% of the observed reduction in industry costs during the study period, which the authors emphasize is a larger effect than that found in previous research.

15

required by ICC/STB case precedent, by regulations for railroad consolidation, and by economic principles.[25] These positions overlap with Department of Justice and Federal Trade Commission antitrust merger guidelines, which require that claimed efficiencies be "merger-specific."[26]

Christensen did not consider many of the methods used to estimate the benefits, or the results, to be well-documented, making it difficult for him to verify or replicate the results. He conceded that the public benefits could be as high as $505 million in a normal year (as compared to the applicants' $750.6 million figure) but also argued that the benefits could be as low as $73 million. The largest claimed benefit, labor cost savings, was scaled down considerably in Christensen's analysis by subtracting out those savings likely to be attributable to the labor productivity gains (estimated to be 2.4% annually) he expected to occur industry-wide, in any event, for the relevant time period. He was inclined to discount the shipper logistics savings because (1) some savings would probably be realized in any event as industry-wide productivity gains occur, (2) the underlying traffic diversion models were not well documented, and (3) the diversion estimates reflected a subjective "consensus" opinion.[27] Christensen criticized the

---

[25]Department of Justice, Brief Before the Surface Transportation Board (June 3, 1996), DOJ-14 in *Union Pacific Corp. – Control & Merger – Southern Pacific Corp.*, STB Finance Docket 32760, at 43.

[26]The antitrust agencies "will consider only those efficiencies likely to be accomplished with the proposed merger and unlikely to be accomplished in the absence of the proposed merger or another means having comparable anticompetitive effects." Moreover, merger-specific efficiencies must be verifiable to be "cognizable" under antitrust merger guidelines. See DOJ/FTC (1992, revised 1997) § 4. There is less overlap between regulatory and antitrust standards for mergers along other dimensions. For example, the STB appears to recognize fixed as well as variable cost savings but efficiencies are more likely to be considered cognizable under DOJ/FTC merger guidelines if they represent marginal cost reductions. See DOJ/FTC (1992, revised 1997) § 4.

[27]Merger applicants used two transportation consulting firms, Transmode Consultants and Reebie Associates, to project traffic diversions of truckload shipments to UP/SP intermodal (truck/rail) service, due to merger-related service improvements in several traffic corridors, and to estimate associated logistics cost savings to shippers. Transmode Consultants did this with a computer-based "logistics cost diversion model" and data from the North American Truck Survey (compiled by the Association of American Railroads). Reebie Associates used a different methodology and data source, which led to somewhat different results. The two consulting firms conferred to reach agreement on "best estimates" of traffic diversion. Transmode Consultants separately used a variation of its logistics cost diversion model to estimate costs savings (due to merger-related savings in time and mileage) to UP/SP shippers presently using SP for rail carload traffic between selected points in the West. See verified statement of Don P. Ainsworth (Reebie Associates), in Union Pacific Corporation and Southern Pacific Corporation, UP/SP-22, "Railroad Merger Application" (November 30, 1995), Vol. 1, at 433-463, in *Union Pacific Corp. - Control and Merger - Southern Pacific Corp.*, STB Finance Docket 32760; and verified statement of Paul O. Roberts (Transmode Consultants), in the same volume, at 465-485.

inclusion of net revenue gains, trackage rights proceeds, and procurement savings because, in his view, these were transfers generating private but not social benefits. He also did not consider the merger to be necessary for achieving efficiencies in the areas of operation, general and administrative, communications/computers, and freight car utilization.

The STB was influenced by these arguments. Its review of the claimed benefits, and its consideration of opposing arguments from DOJ/Christensen and others, led to the downward adjustment of public benefits shown in Table 3 on the next page. That is, applicants' claimed benefits for a normal year were scaled down from $750.6 million to $627.4 million, a 16.4% reduction. Likewise, the STB's figure for operating benefits, $534.3 million, was lower (by 8.5%) than the claimed operating benefits of $583.8 million. The restated $534.3 million in operating benefits was achievable, according to the Board, because:

> UP/SP will: (a) streamline and consolidate operations at major common terminals; (b) combine terminal and station facilities at a number of common points; (c) establish new blocks and new trains to improve service and efficiency; and (d) pursue numerous coordinations and consolidations of transportation, mechanical, engineering, information, purchasing, customer service, and other operating and marketing functions and activities. In addition, traffic will be handled more efficiently, in many instances by using shorter routes. The combined car fleet will be managed on a coordinated basis to reduce empty movements and improve equipment use. Economies will also be achieved in applicant carriers' administrative functions by combining SP and UP departments to permit more efficient use of existing personnel and reduce overall staff and office space.[28]

The $534.3 million in efficiency gains, if expressed as a percent of total operating expenses, would be 6.2% for a normal year. The STB concluded from the record that gains of this magnitude, ceteris paribus, would enable the combined railroad to lower its operating ratio – operating expenses as a percent of operating revenues – by at least four points.[29]

Table 3

STB Restatement of Applicants' Projected
Annual Efficiencies and Cost Savings for Normal Year
($ in millions)

---

[28]Surface Transportation Board, 1 S.T.B. 233 (1996), at 376.

[29]1 S.T.B. 233 (1996), at 376 and Appendix F: Financial Ratios, at 576-577. The operating ratio is a frequently used efficiency measure in the railroad industry, despite obvious shortcomings. In the pre-merger year of 1995, UP's operating ratio was 79.2% while SP's was 96.7%. The S.T.B.'s Appendix F table shows the combined railroad's operating ratio falling from 82.9% to 78.9% by the fifth year of merger implementation.

Operating Benefits	
Labor Savings	$261.2
Non-Labor Savings	
Car Use	12.7
Communications/Computers	14.2
Operations	116.5
General/Administrative	129.7
Subtotal (Operating Benefits)	534.3
Shipper Logistics Savings	93.1
Total Quantifiable Benefits	$627.4

Source: Surface Transportation Board, *Union Pacific/Southern Pacific Merger*, 1 S.T.B. 233 (1996), table at 376.

The STB's assessment of these issues appears to have been generally sound, with certain exceptions. The agency appropriately excluded $47.2 million in net trackage rights proceeds from BNSF (included in operations savings) because the largest portion of it appeared to be a transfer. It also appropriately excluded the $76 million in net revenue gains because traffic diversions, as such, are not public benefits. The cost savings and service improvements that lead to traffic diversions are accounted for elsewhere. More difficult to assess is the STB's rejection of Christensen's argument that $102.9 million in procurement savings (from combined purchases) is a transfer from suppliers to UP/SP, and not reflective of efficiencies achieved by suppliers. Christensen had the better of the argument to the extent such savings merely reflect UP/SP's combined purchasing power. Yet, it does seem that combining procurement functions had the potential to save resources for UP/SP, and that volume discounts could, to some extent, reflect real economies for suppliers.

The STB found that claimed efficiency benefits – particularly labor savings – were not based on continuing productivity improvements in the substantially deregulated environment following enactment of the 1980 Staggers Rail Act,[30] as DOJ/Christensen had argued, but on particular savings made possible by implementation of the post-merger operating plan.

---

[30]For an examination of productivity improvements and cost reductions that were facilitated by Staggers-related regulatory reforms, see Jerry Ellig, "Railroad Deregulation and Consumer Welfare." *Journal of Regulatory Economics* 21 (2002), 143-167.

Christensen admitted he had not examined the operating plan.[31] It does not appear, however, that the STB otherwise attempted to verify the labor savings results, so one can reasonably question whether they would be as high as the $261 million in a normal year claimed by the applicants and accepted by the STB.

The Board also considered the shipper logistics savings to be merger-related, rather than reflective of ongoing productivity gains for the entire industry, as Christensen had urged. The underlying traffic diversion model employed by Transmode Consultants to generate the savings estimates was explained by Transmode to have been developed for the Federal Railroad Administration, and widely used. Nevertheless, Christensen was correct in arguing that its use here was not well-documented in the merger application and, as a result, its findings and the consensus estimates were difficult to verify.[32] Moreover, the shipper logistics savings of $93.1 million shown in the STB's restatement appears to double-count part of the cost savings reported under total operating benefits. That is, cost savings from single-line service and more efficient routes are counted as operating benefits to the combined railroad, and counted again (at least for the subset of traffic corridors examined in the diversion analysis) as savings to shippers.

As for DOJ/Christensen's argument that some or all of the benefits in operations, general and administrative, communications/computers, and car utilization could be achieved through arrangements short of merger, the STB responded that it and the Interstate Commerce Commission historically were inclined to show deference to rail management as to how efficiencies can best be achieved. The Board cited earlier decisions where applicants explored at length non-merger alternatives suggested by DOJ, and the Board concluded there were "practical, legal, and competitive problems which would substantially lessen the effectiveness of such arrangements."[33] The Board found in these cases that unified management resulting from a merger was necessary to attain significant operating economies projected in the merger applications, and the STB seemed to have a reasonable basis for its decisions in these matters.[34]

---

[31]The STB was also critical of the method Christensen used to scale down the labor savings estimate because that estimate was attributed to observed labor productivity gains in the industry for 1989-94. This was a period of time, however, when the positive effects on productivity of several rail mergers, as well as other industry-wide innovations, were likely to have occurred.

[32]The Reebie Associates methodology for estimating traffic diversion and shipper cost savings is even less apparent from its description in the merger application.

[33]Surface Transportation Board, 1 S.T.B. 233 (1996), at 379.

[34]UP argued that cooperation works best when two railroads are "similarly motivated and are prepared to commit equal resources – preconditions that rarely apply in practice." UP illustrates problems it had encountered, attempting to enter into cooperative arrangements with SP, with an example of failed efforts over the years to rationalize their train operations between Salt Lake City and Ogden UT, a congested segment of each railroad's route between the Midwest and West Coast. The consequences for each railroad were delay, extra fuel cost, and additional miles for each train traveling the route. The inability to reach an agreement was

The Board also noted that voluntary arrangements short of merger would not confer the antitrust immunity that an STB-approved merger provides; which is particularly important for a UP/SP-type merger where the "core operations of their competing systems" need to be coordinated.[35]

C. Assessment of STB Review of Unquantified Benefits

Turning to the unquantified benefits, the STB concluded its review of the record by stating that the merger applicants had provided evidence of "unprecedented opportunities for improved routings and new single-line routes."[36] As in past rail merger cases, the STB placed substantial weight on evidence of improved routes, and consistently recognized single-line service to be a public benefit.

Christensen had argued that there are a number of ways railroads can cooperate for mutual gain that do not involve merging. Examples given include the grant of trackage rights, run-through trains,[37] and the leasing of idle cars to railroads with car shortages.[38] Thus, some of the claimed benefits could be achieved, according to Christensen, by means short of merger. The STB responded, it seems appropriately given the practical, legal and competitive problems it had experienced with non-merger alternatives, that it is implausible that coordination on this scale could be achieved through voluntary trackage rights and other cooperative arrangements, and not require the impetus of merger.[39]

---

attributed to the cost of resolving labor issues; its impact on the relative competitiveness of the two rival carriers; UP's doubts about SP's willingness to maintain and upgrade its tracks on the route; and difficult compensation issues because the two routes were of different length and had different maintenance requirements. See UP/SP-24 (1995) at 9-15. Nevertheless, Christensen took the view that arrangements short of merger generally were feasible, suggesting somewhat implausibly, for example, that it would be a simple matter for SP to gain access to UP's superior Transportation Communications System software by contracting with UP, its rival, for it. See Christensen (1996), at 31-32.

[35]Surface Transportation Board, 1 S.T.B. 233 (1996), at 379.

[36]1 S.T.B. 233 (1996), at 381.

[37]This is an arrangement that allows a railroad to assemble a train of cars in a manner that avoids or reduces intermediate switching by another railroad in an interline movement. The locomotive as well as the cars are interchanged between the two railroads.

[38]Likewise, Massa (1997), at 432, cites a number of examples, since the early 1990s, of voluntary trackage or hauling arrangements, and joint marketing agreements, that purportedly were implemented in the absence of merger.

[39]There is an apparent inconsistency, as noted for example by Massa (1997), at 440-441, in the STB finding non-merger arrangements such as trackage rights to be infeasible, and the Board accepting trackage rights as a workable merger remedy. One significant and obvious

While the Board's treatment of expanded single-line service and more efficient routes as unquantified benefits suggests they should be considered in addition to quantified benefits, they are more properly regarded as a restatement of cost savings for the combined railroad, which are counted under operating benefits. That is, merger-related cost savings are passed on to shippers to some extent but the savings to shippers are not quantified by merger applicants, except, as discussed above, for those captured in the shipper logistics savings.

Other unquantified benefits highlighted by the STB include capital expenditures to be undertaken by the combined railroad to improve service and enhance competitive effectiveness. The Board considered them to be merger-related investments, as the details of the merger application operating plan suggest. Many of the investments were intended to update what the STB characterized as SP's inadequate rail lines and related structures and facilities. The Board concluded, and the record seems to support, that SP could not raise the capital for this task on its own, and UP, not unreasonably, would lack the motivation to provide such capital through any arrangement short of merger.[40]

While the projected capital expenditures appear to be merger related, they should not in and of themselves be regarded as public benefits. If undertaken as planned, they could lead to public benefits, properly measured as cost reductions, cost savings and service improvements, but they are the predicate for those benefits. In other words, they should be viewed as costs of achieving the claimed operating benefits, and the merger applicants elsewhere treated them as

---

difference, however, is that trackage rights as a merger remedy would be negotiated by the parties, because they are mandated, and that the STB would have continuing oversight. In addition, the STB took steps to resolve predictable problems associated with trackage rights agreements in this context. As one example, the STB had the merger applicants and BN/SF reach a written agreement on a protocol to prevent discrimination by UP/SP train dispatchers against BN/SF trains in gaining access to UP/SP's rail lines (see 1 S.T.B. 233 (1996), at 403-404, and Conant (2004), at 126). The STB also had in place procedures for setting compensation rates for the trackage rights to ensure they were adequate as reimbursement to an owner railroad such as UP/SP but would not preclude a tenant railroad such as BN/SF from being an effective competitor (see 1 S.T.B. 233 (1996), at 413-417). In general, the STB noted that trackage rights had been widely used and time tested in rail merger proceedings (see 1 S.T.B. 233 (1996), at 371) . While these differences resolve some of the apparent inconsistency, they also suggest that trackage rights in the merger context may not be free from regulatory burden or error.

[40]Funds from internal SP sources or public capital markets were reported to be increasingly difficult to obtain to meet SP's capital shortfall. This is not to suggest some sort of capital market failure but rather that the efficiencies and service improvements for which capital improvements were needed were in areas requiring cooperation between UP and SP to achieve them. The STB found that UP was the only railroad offering to acquire the entire SP system and invest the amounts needed, and UP attributed this willingness to the "unique synergies" it saw flowing from combining the two systems. See verified statement of Lawrence C. Yarberry on behalf of Union Pacific Corporation and Southern Pacific Corporation in UP/SP-22, "Railroad Merger Application" (November30, 1995), Vol. 1, at 260, in *Union Pacific Corp. - Control & Merger - Southern Pacific Corp.*, STB Finance Docket 32760.

one-time costs (as explained above with respect to Table 1).

D. Conclusion on Claimed Merger Benefits

UP can be credited with submitting a merger application that enumerated claimed benefits and made reasonable attempts to quantify them in dollar terms. These claims were further supported by UP's merger implementation and operating plan, also submitted as part of the merger application, which provided a detailed explanation of how and when claimed merger benefits were to be achieved. Also to its credit, UP presented claimed benefits net of the costs incurred to achieve them, including required capital expenditures. In addition, claimed benefits that were not quantified were, nonetheless, described and itemized.

The STB appropriately considered not only the magnitude of the claimed benefits and support for the amounts claimed, but also whether they were public rather than private in nature, attributable to the merger, and not reasonably achievable through other means less likely to raise competitive concerns. It did not merely rubber stamp all of the benefits claimed by applicants but at the same time it did not mechanically accept the exclusions proposed by DOJ's witness Christensen. The eventual STB decision suggests that many rail-related efficiency claims can be demonstrated to be merger-specific under regulatory standards and perhaps antitrust standards as well. The Board's exclusion of certain claimed benefits because they appeared to be transfers (private benefits) seems justified, although its decision not to exclude any part of procurement savings from combined purchases, for the same reason, could be questioned. Also questionable was the STB's willingness to accept all of the shipper logistics savings, since some of these seem to double-count savings already listed under operating benefits, and because the method of deriving these savings was not well-documented.

A substantial part, but probably not all, of the claimed savings – particularly labor cost savings – could properly be attributed to the merger, rather than to expected productivity gains in the industry, and it does not seem that integration by other than ownership, at least at that time, was a reasonable alternative to achieving claimed benefits on the scale contemplated by UP. There does appear to be room for improvement in terms of the STB's efforts to verify the estimates (closer inspection of work sheets, etc.). This leaves open the possibility that some exaggeration by merger applicants may have occurred and, because of a national transportation policy still favorable to rail mergers at the time, may have been allowed by the STB.[41] Even if one made adjustments for these considerations, however, the properly recognized (or cognizable) public benefits seem to be of substantial magnitude.

That might actually be an understatement of benefits because the analysis has compared a post-merger outcome with a pre-merger world. To the extent that SP's assets and service levels would have deteriorated without the merger, the merger may have generated greater benefits

---

[41]Regarding its review of future rail mergers under new railroad consolidation procedures, the STB has stated that "we will scrutinize claimed benefits very closely." See Surface Transportation Board, *Major Rail Consolidation Procedures*, STB Ex Parte No. 582 (Sub-No. 1), Decision served June 11, 2001, at 17.

than the present analysis implies. In its 1996 merger decision, the STB did find that SP was financially weak, and that its service level was below that offered by competitors, and declining.[42] As previously noted, the STB concluded that UP was the only buyer to make an offer for the entire SP system.

The STB also examined the unquantified benefits claimed by the merger applicants, and found them to be important public benefits. Unquantified benefits that take the form of expanded single-line service and more efficient routes, however, are the manifestation of the cost savings already accounted for under operating benefits claimed, and those that take the form of capital expenditures may well lead to public benefits but are actually a cost of achieving them.

IV. Evidence on Realization of Claimed Merger Benefits

A. Merger Implementation and Service Disruptions and Delays

The merger was consummated in September 1996, and a multi-stage implementation plan commenced. Months into the merger implementation process, however, press accounts appeared indicating that the UP/SP system was experiencing significant service problems. The GAO later identified July 1997 as the start of serious service disruptions and shipment delays, which continued into 1998.[43] Mounting traffic congestion on what was described as the aging rail infrastructure in the Houston area began affecting rail service throughout the western U.S. Service problems were evident across the UP/SP system and took the form of poor transit times and inadequate car supply. In the first annual oversight hearings (STB-1997) on the UP/SP merger, the Board characterized these service and safety deficiencies as quite serious and took a number of actions to resolve them.[44] The Board found in STB-1997 that the service disruptions were caused by a variety of factors including UP efforts to rehabilitate SP's deteriorating infrastructure and establish facilities that would ultimately mean improved service for shippers,

---

[42]DOJ had taken issue with the claim that SP was financially weak, noting, for example, that SP had generated positive cash flow in three of the previous five years. It also thought that SP's competitive effectiveness should not be ruled out because of it service problems. Claims of inferior service and weak and deteriorating financial condition at the time of the merger, however, were further supported by a subsequent UP report. See verified statement of John T. Gray, in Union Pacific Corporation, UP/SP-384, "Union Pacific's Fifth Annual Oversight Report" (July 2, 2001), public version, in *Union Pacific Corp. - Control & Merger - Southern Pacific Corp.*, STB Finance Docket 32760. See also Conant (2004), at 120, noting that for the years1982-1995, SP revenue from rail operations had exceeded operating expenses just four times.

[43]See General Accounting Office, *Railroad Regulation: Changes in Freight Railroad Rates from 1997 through 2000.* GAO-02-524 (June 2002), at 5-6.

[44]Surface Transportation Board, "Oversight," Decision No. 10, in *Union Pacific Corp.–Control & Merger–Southern Pacific Corp.*, STB Finance Docket 32760 (Sub-No. 21), Decision served October 27, 1997.

and other system integration efforts that had not progressed as they should have. UP acknowledged that difficulty in finalizing labor agreements was delaying implementation of workforce integration, and that installation of a new computerized control network needed to operate the merged system was behind schedule. However, UP also pointed to a number of unrelated events that made service problems worse and that were clearly beyond its control. These ranged from surges in demand for rail transportation and backups in traffic moving to and from Mexico related to rail privatization there, to problems caused by floods and hurricanes. By December 1998, however, in its second oversight hearings decision (STB-1998), the Board concluded that the UP/SP service situation had improved considerably and was expected to continue to improve.[45]

It is undisputed that serious service problems occurred in the post-merger period. Any merger is likely to encounter at least some integration problems, and integration-related reductions in service reliability should be viewed as a disadvantage of the merger. Moreover, the probability of encountering integration problems is likely to be higher for larger scale mergers where substantial long-term integration efficiencies are claimed. Critics of the UP/SP merger have pointed out that UP had difficulty in absorbing the smaller Chicago and North Western Railway in 1995 (the STB admits it was a "rocky experience")[46] – more serious integration problems could be expected for the large-scale UP/SP merger.

While the conventional wisdom appears to be that implementation of the merger plan caused both acute and chronic service problems,[47] the record suggests that serious disruptions had ended and service was returning to normal levels after a little more than a year.[48] Moreover, at least with respect to this merger, management shortcomings in anticipating and resolving integration problems may have been just one of several causes of the service problems. The relatively poor condition of the SP infrastructure and unrelated events may have contributed at least as much to the service disruptions, and there is some plausibility to the suggestion by the STB that SP would have experienced service problems even absent the merger has some

----

[45]Surface Transportation Board, "General Oversight," Decision No. 13, in *Union Pacific Corp.–Control & Merger–Southern Pacific Corp.*, STB Finance Docket 32760 (Sub-No. 21). Decision served December 21, 1998.

[46]Surface Transportation Board, 1 S.T.B. 233 (1996), at 378.

[47]This view is reflected in the press, in academic work, and in other commentary. See, respectively, (1) Peter Kaplan, "Grappling with Gridlock," *Washington Times*, December 3, 1997, p. B7; (2) Kwoka and White (2004), Craig W. Conrath and Nicholas A. Widnell, "Efficiency Claims in Merger Analysis: Hostility or Humility?" *George Mason Law Review* 7, (1999), 685-705, White (2002); and (3) Russell Pittman, "Train Wreck: A Lesson in Megamergers," manuscript, June 1, 1998, and Henry B. McFarland, "The Union Pacific–Southern Pacific Merger: What Can Be Learned?" *The Transportation Antitrust Update* (Spring 1999), 5-10.

[48]See, for example, DOT letter dated August 16, 1999, for the 1999 oversight hearings, stating that UP rail service had returned to normal levels. Referenced in STB-1999, at 16.

plausibility.

B. Overview of Realized Merger Benefits

The STB's annual oversight hearings (1997-2001) on the UP/SP merger were initially thought to be a valuable source of public information for research on the extent to which claimed benefits are realized. The merger appeared to be an excellent candidate for a retrospective case study and provide an unusual opportunity to track merger efficiencies all the way from those claimed in a merger application to those achieved post-merger. Unfortunately, progress reports on the realization of projected merger benefits were given relatively little attention in the five post-merger oversight proceedings because the STB was preoccupied with assessing the adequacy of the conditions it imposed on the merger to address competitive concerns,[49] and with resolving the 1997-98 service disruptions and delays. What attention was paid to the realization of merger benefits is summarized below.

The Board, in STB-1998, noted that while the merger has not proceeded as smoothly as expected, it had produced and would continue to produce benefits to the shipping public. Examples given included expansion in the number of single-line services and shorter routings, better equipment deployment, and reduced switching charges. STB-1999[50] discusses the significant progress made in merger implementation during the year. Relying on UP's submission, the STB lists, as examples, the successfully installed Transportation Control System, progress on integration of work forces, and consolidation and improvement of terminals and yards. STB-2000's discussion of merger benefits highlights UP's progress in making capital improvements to rehabilitate SP.[51] UP planned to spend about $1.3 billion over a four year

---

[49]Following the first annual round of oversight hearings, the STB concluded that the record to that point did not reflect any "serious competitive problems." The Board acknowledged, however, it was too early to conclude with any certainty that competition between UP/SP and BN/SF would be vigorous over the longer run. See Surface Transportation Board, "Oversight," Decision No. 10, in *Union Pacific Corp.–Control & Merger–Southern Pacific Corp.*, STB Finance Docket 32760 (Sub-No. 21), at 2. Decision served October 27, 1997. By the fifth and final oversight hearing, the STB concluded more strongly that "overall, the evidence demonstrates that the [trackage rights] conditions we imposed on the UP/SP merger have effectively remedied ... any competitive harm that would otherwise have been associated with that transaction." See Surface Transportation Board, "General Oversight," Decision No. 21 in *Union Pacific Corp.–Control & Merger–Southern Pacific Corp.*, STB Finance Docket 32760 (Sub-No. 21), at 1. Decision served December 20, 2001.

[50]Surface Transportation Board, "General Oversight," Decision No. 15, in *Union Pacific Corp.–Control & Merger–Southern Pacific Corp.*, STB Finance Docket 32760 (Sub-No. 21). Decision served November 30, 1999.

[51]Surface Transportation Board, "General Oversight," Decision No. 16, in *Union Pacific Corp.–Control & Merger–Southern Pacific Corp.*, STB Finance Docket 32760 (Sub-No. 21). Decision served December 15, 2000.

period and reported it was on target since it would spend $1.25 billion by the end of 2000. The Board considered it both burdensome and unnecessary to undertake a study requested by the California Public Utilities Commission to determine whether UP achieved all projected merger benefits and whether the realized benefits had been passed on to shippers. It pointed out the absence of shipper testimony to the contrary and cited an STB staff study finding rate reductions for Western railroads over the years as an indication that efficiency gains were being realized and that many of them were being passed on to shippers.

In the fifth and final oversight proceeding (STB-2001), the STB concurred in UP's assertion that it had achieved the full measure of the merger-related efficiencies predicted and that savings were being passed on to shippers. The public version of the UP submission,[52] however, offers only a few examples of expanded single-line service and shorter routes, and its estimate of annual savings of $690 million from the merger is offered without supporting documentation. Thus, any conclusion that the merging parties substantially achieved the promised service improvements and cost savings must be a preliminary one, to the extent it is based on the public record from the STB's post-merger oversight proceedings.

C. Realization of Quantified Benefits

To further document the realization of claimed merger benefits, several additional sources of public and non-public information were consulted. Public sources include UP presentations to financial analysts; merger-related commentary in UP reports to the Securities and Exchange Commission (SEC); and relevant academic research. Public information on post-merger operating ratios, rates, and customer (shipper) satisfaction was also considered as possible indirect evidence of realized merger benefits. Non-public sources of information include (1) UP's internal tracking report on the realization of merger efficiencies, which was especially relevant for this report, (2) the confidential version of UP's submission (UP/SP-384) for the STB's 2001 oversight hearings (covering post-merger service improvements, capital expenditures, and UP's rate study),[53] and (3) customer satisfaction surveys conducted by UP. The non-public documents were obtained from attorneys at Covington & Burling, serving as outside counsel for UP. The attorneys also briefed the author on those documents and were available then and at other times to answer questions about them. These documents were supplied voluntarily, but the author is not aware what other relevant information, whether favorable or not to UP, may have existed.

Table 4 presents the results of an effort by UP to track the realization of merger efficiencies for management purposes, and it shows that substantial ongoing benefits were achieved. The "ongoing savings" line corresponds to "operating benefits" in applicants' Table 1

---

[52]Union Pacific Corporation, UP/SP-384, "Union Pacific's Fifth Annual Oversight Report" (July 2, 2001), public version, in *Union Pacific Corp. - Control & Merger - Southern Pacific Corp.*, STB Finance Docket 32760.

[53]Confidential submissions in the merger proceedings were available under STB rules to outside counsel and consultants to parties to the proceedings.

and STB's Table 3 and the $679 million in realized savings in fixed and variable costs exceed the normal-year operating benefits of $583.8 million, as claimed by applicants, and restated as $534.3 million by the STB. The outside attorneys represent that UP management sought post-merger progress reports on merger-specific savings to compare to its multi-stage merger

Table 4

Merger Benefits and Costs
Ongoing Merger Benefits
($ in Millions)

	1997	1998	1999	2000	2001
Material / Contract Prices	$31	$48	$47	$49	$49
Operational Savings	60	167	196	247	268
Labor Savings	72	142	171	254	257
All Other - Net of Costs	79	82	105	105	105
Ongoing Savings - Net	242	439	519	655	679
Commodity Revenue - (Est)	–	–	–	90	150
Total Ongoing Benefits	242	439	519	745	829

Source: Union Pacific document provided to the author by Covington & Burling.

implementation plan. The tracking and reporting were done by the Financial Analysis Group in UP's Finance Department and the results were reviewed by senior management. Department heads, who assisted in identifying merger benefits, reportedly had little incentive to overstate them as their budgets normally were reduced by the merger benefit amounts. These considerations give the numbers greater credibility than they would have if they had been generated exclusively for regulatory purposes, such as for presentation during STB's post-merger annual oversight proceedings.[54] UP, of course, would have an incentive to report favorable information publicly, in an appropriate format, and it did report a total operating savings figure in the public version of its UP/SP-384 (2001) submission for the STB's final oversight hearing.[55] At one point, it also reported favorable information about realized merger

---

[54]Consistent with this change in purpose, note that shipper logistics savings do not appear in Table 4 even though they were claimed as a benefit in Table 1.

[55]According to outside counsel for UP, the operating savings figure of $679 million in Table 4 for 2001 (current as of October 2000) was updated to $690 million, as noted above, for UP's July 2001 submission to the STB.

efficiencies to securities analysts.[56]

According to outside counsel for UP, the numbers for material/contract prices in Table 4 reflect discounts on fuel and materials, and similar savings on supply/service contracts.[57] (The material/contract price category was included in general/administrative in Table 1.) To the extent the discounts on combined purchases reflect cost savings to suppliers, they are public benefits.

The sources for the operational savings numbers in the table are numerous. Consistent with the merger-related operating plan, they include shorter routes, directional running, reduced interchange of cars between railroads, enhanced car utilization (listed separately in Table 1), combined freight yards and freight car shops, and combined offices and computer systems.[58] The merger also provided an opportunity to introduce a hub and spoke system for deploying train crews. That is, wherever each railroad had a major terminal, train crews were combined into a single workforce with crews assigned to any spoke as needed, as compared to labor's insistence in the past that crews be dedicated to specific routes.[59]

---

[56]In January 1997, at a meeting in New York, UP told rail industry stock analysts that it expected merger-related savings to exceed those quantified in the merger application. As a result, analysts raised their expectations for total operating benefits to $233 million for 1997. For management purposes, UP then tracked actual savings to see how well the company did each year in meeting the new expectations of the stock analysts. As the following non-public table shows, analysts' expectations were not met in 1998, 1999, or 2000, but scaled-down expectations were met in 2001.

Total Ongoing Benefits (millions of $)

	1997	1998	1999	2000	2001
Stock Analysts Expectations	233	510	680	780	820
Actual Benefits	242	439	519	745	829

Source: Union Pacific document provided to the author by Covington & Burling.

[57]The author did not have full access to the information underlying the entries in Table 4.

[58]Itemization of operational savings shown for 2000, for example, would include, among other items, savings associated with elimination of interchanges and improved car utilization amounting to $35 million, and savings associated with the directional operation of trains amounting to $18 million. (Net trackage rights proceeds were disallowed by the STB, for reasons given above, and are excluded from the operational savings reported in Table 4.)

[59]UP also cited operational savings (but not dollar amounts) in its periodic reports to the SEC. Its annual report for 1997, for example, mentions the following ongoing elements of integration: (1) introduction of directional operation on parallel tracks in certain corridors, (2) negotiation and implementation of labor agreements to allow more efficient use of train crews in

Labor cost savings, as shown in Table 4, were reportedly achieved in every department, and most of the redundant workforce eliminated involved other than train crews. (Some of these savings were accounted for under general/administrative in Table 1.) According to 10-K (annual) and 10-Q (quarterly) reports UP submitted to the SEC, the merger implementation plan called for severing 5,200 employees. Its quarterly reports to the SEC reported progress toward that goal, e.g., 2,450 severed by the first quarter of 1999, 3,620 severed by the third quarter of 2000, and its annual report for 2001 indicates that it completed elimination of the 5,200 employees.

Labor protection/separation costs paid during the merger implementation period reportedly were subtracted from the labor savings on an as-paid basis. These expenditures, however, represent transfer payments from the railroad to employees and, as such, should not be subtracted from the real resource savings associated with the elimination of a redundant workforce. Their inclusion leads to an understatement of labor savings in an unknown amount. If the labor protection/separation projections of Table 1 are any guide, however, the understatement over a five-year merger implementation period would be almost $190 million.

The "all other" savings in Table 4 reflect net savings from eliminating outsourcing of SP's computer systems and enhancing UP's systems (listed separately in Table 1 as communications/computers). It also reflects savings from combining headquarters functions in such areas as insurance, leases, warranties, and finance (which together appeared in general/administrative in Table 1). The commodity revenue entry in the table is not recognized here because it is the net revenue gains item that was rejected as a public benefit by the STB for reasons given above.

Recent academic research also suggests that rail mergers have produced efficiency gains. Wilson and Bitzan (2003) estimated a railroad cost function for the period 1983-1997 and then simulated industry costs to evaluate the changing industry structure.[60] Their basic finding is that merger-related consolidation during the study period produced substantial cost savings. UP/SP is one of eleven rail mergers studied and among the eight for which cost savings were observed.

---

hub and spoke operations, and (3) integration of computer systems. See Union Pacific Railroad Company, "Annual Report to the Securities and Exchange Commission," Form 10-K for fiscal year ended December 31, 1997, at 3. Its 1998 quarterly reports indicate that UP continued to merge or dispose of redundant facilities, cancel uneconomical and duplicative SP contracts, and dispose of certain rail lines. UP also noted that full implementation of the merger will result in expanded single-line service, shorter routes, faster transit times, better on-time performance, and more efficient traffic flow. See, for example, Union Pacific Railroad Company, "Quarterly Report to the Securities and Exchange Commission," Form 10-Q for the quarter ending June 30, 1998, at 11.

[60]Merger-related changes in railroad costs were simulated by comparing predicted post-merger costs of the combined railroad, using observed values for network/operating characteristics, factor prices, scale, and output, with the same post-merger cost function evaluated at the pre-merger values of the railroads' variables the year before they merged.

The robustness of the Wilson and Bitzan finding for the UP/SP merger, however, is open to question because the only post-merger data included are for 1997. This was relatively early in the merger implementation plan and it was an unusual year because of the service disruptions. Wilson and Bitzan decomposed total merger-related cost changes into their sources – for UP/SP the predicted $137.8 million in cost savings reflects certain cost-reducing factors (e.g., lower output and reduced network size) outweighing certain cost-increasing factors (e.g., lower average train speed). Lower output and train speed, however, may be symptomatic of the service disruptions and delays experienced in 1997.[61] It would be desirable to add data to the study sample for additional years following the UP/SP merger to clarify the initial finding of costs savings for that rail merger.

Finally, if ongoing savings were increasing as Table 4 indicates, ceteris paribus, one would expect the combined firm's operating ratio to be declining during the post-merger period. In fact, the combined firm's operating ratio rose from 79.1% in 1996 to 87.4% in 1997, and to 95.4% in 1998 before falling to 82.0% in 1999, 82.3% in 2000, and 80.7% in 2001.[62] Obviously the projected four point reduction in operating ratio was not achieved, but the impact of the merger on that ratio was obscured by other factors affecting operating revenues and operating expenses. Chief among these, as reported to the SEC, were the service problems of 1997-98 that decreased operating revenues and increased operating expenses. In its annual report to the SEC for 1999, UP management did credit increased operating efficiency and service levels and benefits of continuing integration of SP as a reason for operating expenses falling and the operating ratio improving.[63] The operating ratio is also adversely affected by periods of significantly higher fuel costs, as was reported to be the case in 2000.[64]

---

[61]As a rough comparison, one could compare the $137.8 million figure (for 1997) with the merger applicants' claimed operating benefits for Year 1 (approximately 1997) of the five-year merger implementation plan. Table 1 above shows annual operating benefits (less net revenue gains) to be $217.0 million ($239.8 million minus $22.8 million) for Year 1. As a projection, that figure does not include any ongoing cost impact of service problems actually experienced in 1997. Service disruption-related cost increases of a recurring nature would bring the $217 million down closer to the $137.8 million figure.

[62]Union Pacific Corporation, *2001 Annual Report*, at 22-23.

[63]See Union Pacific Railroad Company, "Annual Report to the Securities and Exchange Commission," Form 10-K for fiscal year ending December 31, 1999, at 22. Similarly, Conant (2004), at 129, attributes UP/SP's 1999 and 2000 financial recovery, from service disruptions and delays, to completion of merger-related capital investments in rail lines and acquisition of locomotives.

[64]Sun and Tang examined financial measures/operating performance, pre- and post-merger, for 13 rail mergers occurring in 1976-1996, including the UP/SP merger. One measure tested was operating margin, which can be shown to equal 1.0 minus the operating ratio. They found that operating performance declined (i.e., operating ratio increased) during the first two years following a merger. The results for UP/SP were not stated separately but even if the outcome was the same, it would not be particularly surprising. First, the UP/SP service problems

D. Realization of Unquantified Benefits

1. Expanded Single-Line Service and Improved Routings

Regarding service improvements, UP reported during the 2001 STB oversight hearings (STB-2001) that every shipper on the former UP system that did not already have SP as well as UP service, now has single-line service to every SP point.[65] Likewise, every shipper on the former SP system that did not already have UP as well as SP service, now has single-line service to every UP point. Examples include (1) lumber from UP origins in WA and ID to SP points throughout CA, AZ, NM, and TX, and (2) grains from UP origins in IA, NE, and MN to AZ, and the San Joaquin and Imperial Valleys of CA.

Table 5 on the next page provides a number of examples of expanded single-line service and improved routings taken from an appendix to UP's submission for the 2001 oversight hearings. The examples indicate the merger-related changes giving rise to the service improvements and they identify the positive impact on the shippers affected. Elsewhere in UP/SP-384 (2001), the implementation of directional operations is discussed, e.g., pairing UP

Table 5

Examples of Expanded Single-Line Service and Improved Routings

---

occurred during the first two post-merger years. Second, UP/SP merger implementation was intended to take more than two years. See Huey-Lian Sun and Alex P. Tang, "The Sources of Railroad Merger Gains: Evidence from Stock Price Reaction and Operating Performance," *Transportation Journal* 39 (Summer 2000), 14-26.

[65]UP/SP-384 (2001), public version at 33-34.

Amoco and Centennial Gas, LPG, 900 cars, UP Wyoming origins to Calexico CA (SP). Reduced rates on new single-line service allowed UP Wyoming LPG producers to market their product in western Mexico via SP's Calexico gateway on the border.

Anheuser Busch, malt, 940 cars, Idaho Falls ID (UP) to Van Nuys CA (SP). Traffic had been moving UP-Ogden-SP. UP reduced rates to reflect single-line service and a shorter route.

ARCH Coal, Inc., Canyon Fuels Co., and other Utah coal producers, coal, 33174 cars, Utah origins to Los Angeles for export. The merged system single-line route saves 470 miles over SP's pre-merger route. Rates have been reduced and traffic has grown substantially.

California Portland Cement, coal, 2,510 cars, Skyline UT (SP) to Colton (UP, SP) and Creal CA (SP). The merger created a new single-line route for this traffic more than 465 miles shorter than SP's previous route. UP reduced rates to Colton and to Creal to reflect its ability to move the traffic using the shorter route.

Chevron, petroleum oil, 200 cars, Port Allen LA (UP, KCS) to Richmond CA (SP, BNSF). Before the merger, this traffic had been moving UP-Sweetwater TX-BNSF. The merger made it possible for UP to offer new single-line service and capture this business at a lower rate than the previous joint-line rate.

Eastman Chemical, chemicals, 170 cars, Kingsport TN (NS) to San Pedro CA (SP, BNSF). The traffic had been moving NS-BNSF. UP was able to capture this traffic using its improved Southern Corridor route, which combines UP's line to El Paso with the former SP line to southern California.

Elf Atochem, caustic soda, 110 cars, TG Soda WY (UP) to American OR (BNSF, SP). This traffic shifted from UP-Portland-BNSF to UP direct and Elf Atochem saved on freight costs and enjoyed faster transit times as compared to the pre-merger joint-line route.

Great Western Malting, malt, 1300 cars, Vancouver WA (UP, BNSF) to Fairfield (San Francisco Bay Area) (SP) and Van Nuys (Los Angeles Basin) (SP). After the merger, this traffic shifted from BNSF-Portland-SP to UP direct, with its expanded single-line-service in the I-5 Corridor, at a savings to the customer.

Intermodal (trailer on flat car), Memphis-CA Corridor. New eastbound service was designed to attract United Parcel Service business from Los Angeles to Atlanta and Jacksonville with fifth-day service. Trains operate over UP lines in Arkansas and Texas and over SP's route from El Paso to Los Angeles, to form the shortest route.

Intermodal, Chicago-Northern California. Expedited service over the most direct combination of UP and SP routes through the Central Corridor.

Tyson, frozen poultry, 100 cars, Texarkana TX (SP) to Seattle WA (UP, BNSF). This traffic shifted from SP-BNSF to UP direct, with its expanded single-line service and a rate reduction per car.

Wheat from western Canada, 400 cars, Eastport WA (CP, UP) to various Arizona and California destinations (SP). As a result of the merger, the new single-line UP movement allows for more efficient operations and competitive rates.

Source: UP/SP-384, "Union Pacific's Fifth Annual Oversight Report" (July 2, 2001), Appendix A, in *Union Pacific Corp. - Control & Merger - Southern Pacific Corp.*, STB Finance Docket 32760.

and SP lines from St. Louis and Memphis to the Rio Grande into more efficient directional railroads that save investment dollars and speed shipments.[66] Public versions of these and other

---

[66]UP/SP-384 (2001), public version at 35.

examples of service improvements were highlighted by UP in its presentations to financial analysts.[67] Presumably these examples are verifiable and as such provide some confirmation for claimed merger efficiencies.

More recently, amid an STB-imposed moratorium on rail mergers, railroads reportedly have entered into alliances as an alternative to end-to-end mergers to extend single-line service, thereby casting some doubt on the continuing necessity of ownership integration to achieve these efficiencies.[68] UP itself is now on record asserting that many claimed benefits of recent end-to-end mergers (e.g., BN/SF, UP/Missouri Pacific) might well have been achieved through means short of merger.[69] UP gives as an example "long-term alliances to coordinate interline operations," made possible by rapid advances in information technology "to achieve benefits traditionally attributed to end-to-end mergers."[70] In fact, UP has sought to improve interline service by entering into such alliances with Canadian Pacific, Canadian National, CSX, and Norfolk Southern.[71] The STB has declared in its new railroad consolidation procedures that it will consider more closely whether claimed benefits could be achieved by means other than the proposed merger before it. And it did find that initiatives such as "interline partnerships" can produce many of the efficiencies of a merger while risking less harm.[72] The STB's action provides an additional incentive for potential merger partners to consider alternatives, although it is not a market-generated incentive.

2. Increased Capacity and Capital Investment

UP ended up making about the capital expenditures it estimated. It had projected undertaking $1.3 billion in capital expenditures to implement the operating plan for the merger.

---

[67]See, for example, Brad King, Union Pacific Executive Vice President, "Network Optimization," Presentation to Securities Analysts, New York City (November 28-29, 2001). Mr King conceded that some service improvements noted in the merger application had yet to be implemented, e.g., single-line service through the mountain states linking Texas and the Pacific Northwest, and that directional operations had proved feasible so far only in the South Central region, as just noted.

[68]Daniel Machalaba, "Railroads Are Entering Alliances in Effort to Increase Efficiency," *Wall Street Journal,* May 24, 2001.

[69]UP does not make this argument for parallel mergers, which is how it distinguishes the UP/SP merger. That merger according to UP, sought to improve service by eliminating redundancies in facilities and costs in geographic areas where overlaps existed. This is in contrast to an end-to-end merger's focus on geographic extensions of service.

[70]Union Pacific Corporation, Comments of Union Pacific Corporation and Union Pacific Railroad Company Before the Surface Transportation Board, in *Public Views of Major Rail Consolidations*, STB Ex Parte No. 582 (February 29, 2000), at 10.

[71]King (2001).

[72]Surface Transportation Board, *Major Rail Consolidation Procedures* (2001), at 16.

In the STB's 2000 oversight hearing decision (STB (2000)), it is reported that by year-end UP would have spent about $1.25 billion.[73] This investment included almost $500 million in rail line upgrades, more than $400 million in capacity expansion projects, more than $100 million in information technology, and almost $45 million to refurbish SP locomotives. In UP/SP-384 (2001) it is reported that by year-end UP would have spent $1.586 billion related to the merger.

While the amount actually invested was of the same order of magnitude initially projected, the project mix had changed. The projected $1.3 billion figure was generated, to a significant extent, from a list of "essential projects" as viewed by SP prior to the merger. Many of these projects were undertaken but at a higher cost than SP had assumed (because SP had underestimated rehabilitation costs and/or projected traffic). For example, spending on SP's Sunset Route, listed in Table 2 above, was by 2001 up to nearly $275 million and still growing as compared to the projected $221.4 million; and the $38.2 million projected for upgrading and rehabilitating SP's Roseville Yard ended up as more than $140 million spent to completely rebuild the yard.

Other projects did not need to be undertaken because the merger provided alternatives apparently not considered at the time of the merger application. For example, the UP OKT Line listed in Table 2 was not upgraded (at a projected cost of $91.5 million) because UP found a better route to upgrade (at a lower cost) for coal trains moving between Wyoming and Texas. Another example is the SP Mococo Line from Table 2, which did not need to be upgraded because a nearby UP line could be used and because of a change in traffic patterns.

While the reallocation of capital expenditures may have led to greater or smaller efficiencies in some areas, as compared to projections in the merger application, it does not appear to have adversely affected the total level of operating benefits for a normal year. These were found by UP to be $679 million (Table 4) as compared to UP's projection of $583.8 million (Table 1) or to the STB's restatement of the projection as $534.3 million (Table 3).

E. Customer Satisfaction Surveys

Ceteris paribus, if ongoing savings were increasing as Table 4 indicates, and being passed on to shippers in the form of rate reductions and service improvements, one would expect shipper satisfaction to be greater in the post-merger period.[74] The service disruptions and delays of 1997-98 obviously are a confounding factor and so an appropriate comparison would need to

---

[73]Surface Transportation Board, "General Oversight," Decision No. 16, in *Union Pacific Corp.–Control & Merger–Southern Pacific Corp.*, STB Finance Docket 32760 (Sub-No. 21), at 13. Decision served December 15, 2000.

[74]A search for information on quantifiable service metrics indicates that neither UP, STB, or the American Association of Railroads has developed service metrics that include a pre-merger benchmark to compare with UP's post-merger experience.

straddle that period.[75] One survey meeting that criterion was done in December 1999 and publicized by the National Industrial Traffic League (NITL), the largest organization of freight transportation shippers.[76] It was designed to compare pre-merger and post-merger quality of service for several railroads involved in mergers since the mid-1990s, including UP/SP. Overall, 184 questionnaires were distributed to NITL members, covering the UP/SP and other rail mergers, and 50 were returned.

The results of the NITL survey appear to be inconsistent with other evidence suggesting merger-related efficiencies and service improvements from the UP/SP merger. For example, of the 47 survey respondents reporting that they used UP/SP service, only 6% rated that service "excellent" for the June-December 1999 period, which was well past the service disruptions of 1997-98. UP/SP service was rated "fair" or "poor" for that period by 55% of respondents. As compared to pre-merger service (first half of 1996) on UP or SP lines, UP/SP service in 1999 was rated the same or worse by, respectively, 94% and 70% of the respondents. UP shippers were also asked to compare transit times (June 1996 v. June 1999) for five representative movements. For the 74 reported movements, transit time increased by 13% from an average of 7.5 days to 8.5 days.

There are a number of reasons to discount these findings, notwithstanding the significance of NITL in the shipping community and the wide reporting of the survey results. First, dissatisfied shippers may have been more inclined to complete the survey. Second, lingering bad feelings about service problems in the West may have influenced the responses. Third, service problems in the East during the survey period may have spilled over to the West, given the integrated nature of rail networks in the U.S. Finally, NITL was not a disinterested party in conducting the survey. In fact, it used the results of its shipper survey in one STB proceeding to make the point that "railroads have a well-defined credibility gap when it comes to promises of shipper benefits from mergers."[77] Conversations with Covington & Burling attorneys indicate that, at the time, NITL was seeking open access to rail service for its members and favorable treatment under the new rail consolidation procedures for future rail mergers.

Another customer satisfaction survey that permits pre- and post-merger comparisons is conducted by UP. As explained by outside counsel for UP, the railroad surveys 200 of its

---

[75] Available service metrics do indicate recovery from service disruptions and delays. In STB-2000, the Board cited UP numbers on average train speed and freight car dwell time (the time freight cars spend in a terminal area), as evidence of significant improvement since the service disruptions and delays. For example, UP data show that average train speed had risen from a service-problem low of 12.0 mph, to 20.0 mph, and average freight car dwell time had fallen from a service-problem high of 43.9 hours, to 26.2 hours.

[76] National Industrial Traffic League (NITL), "Results of December 1999 Rail Merger Survey," appendix to Statement of National Industrial Traffic League Before the Surface Transportation Board, in *Public Views on Major Rail Consolidations*, STB Ex Parte No. 582 (February 29, 2000).

[77] NITL (2000), at 6-7.

customers each month, using 35 questions and seeking responses on a scale of 1 ("very dissatisfied") to 5 ("very satisfied"). The responses appear to be scaled-up by a factor of 20 and averaged over the number of respondents to generate a customer satisfaction index with a maximum value of 100. UP's report to financial analysts in November 2001 includes a chart showing the customer satisfaction index for the period 1988-2001, for the following question: "Overall, how satisfied are you with Union Pacific Railroad?"[78] The index for UP-only for 1995, the year prior to the merger, stood at 81.[79] The reported index for 1996 was a combination of UP's scores for the full year with SP's much lower scores for the fourth quarter. The index for UP/SP for 1996 overall was 75. The index then fell to a service-disruption low of approximately 45 in 1998, and then rose to 79 by November 2001. That is, the customer satisfaction index, at least for the general question posed, shows not only recovery from the service disruptions and delays, but also some improvement from the level that prevailed for UP/SP at the time they merged.

A few other customer satisfaction surveys exist, also painting a more positive picture for UP, but they are limited to service in the post-merger period. For example, the outside attorneys provided a bar graph titled "Closing the Gap: Customer Satisfaction." It is based on a non-public customer survey (conducted by UP) for management purposes and compares UP's performance with that of a close competitor – truckload carriers. The graph covers 1998-2000 and shows customer satisfaction for UP rising and UP catching up with truckload carriers in terms of satisfaction. The results depicted, however, are not documented.

More recently, a securities analyst reported a survey of 800 freight shippers, including those using rail service.[80] UP ranked second (to Canadian National) overall in customer satisfaction. On individual dimensions, UP ranked first in geographic coverage, second in ease of doing business, and third in delivery when expected and speed of delivery/cycle time.[81]

In sum, available evidence on customer satisfaction in the post-merger period is mixed and not particularly reliable or informative. Objective service metrics are not available for the relevant time period, surveys indicating customer dissatisfaction appear to be biased, and surveys

---

[78]Ike Evans, Union Pacific President and COO, "Strategy Recap," Presentation to Securities Analysts, New York City (November 28-29, 2001).

[79]According to Covington & Burling attorneys, SP's index would have been 20 or more points below UP's index during the pre-merger period.

[80]James J. Valentine, "Freight Pulse Survey: Second Round Insights," *Equity Research: Freight Transportation.* Morgan Stanley, January 11, 2002.

[81]Also recently, UP was named by Fortune as the most admired railroad, in terms of innovativeness, employee talent, use of corporate assets, quality of management, quality of products/services, etc. A large-scale survey was conducted of executives directors, and security analysts to determine the scores/rankings for railroads. Customers were not surveyed but several of the criteria are related to good service. See Matthew Boyle, "America's Most Admired Companies," *Fortune*, March 4, 2002.

showing customer satisfaction are not especially informative.

F. Evidence on Post-Merger Rail Rates

If ongoing savings were increasing as Table 4 indicates, and being passed on to shippers, one would expect to observe real rail rates to be declining in the West during the post-merger period. As early as the 1998 oversight hearings, the STB referred to confidential railroad submissions reportedly showing many examples of BNSF winning 2-to-1 traffic from shippers and many examples of rate and service improvements by UP to retain such traffic. Rate reductions for 3-to-2 traffic were also said to be documented. In connection with the STB's annual oversight hearings, UP undertook a more systematic rate study which compared rail rates for key markets each year post-merger with those in a pre-merger period.[82] In its July 2001 submission to the STB, UP reported, and the STB subsequently accepted, that UP rates had either fallen or remained the same in every relevant market over the multi-year period.[83] This is confirmed by examination of the rate appendix to that submission, which was made available to the author, with UP's approval, by its outside attorneys. The rate comparisons cover 2-to-1 shippers (including and excluding the largest shipper in the Central Corridor), 3-to-2 shippers (auto, intermodal, and general carload), and the following key commodities and traffic corridors: eastern Mexican gateway traffic, Utah and Colorado coal, Gulf Coast plastics, other Gulf Coast chemicals and petroleum products, chemicals and petroleum products generally, and grain. For example, rates for Utah and Colorado Coal traffic held steady while those for traffic moving in the Houston-Memphis and Houston-New Orleans 2-to-1 corridors declined 10.3%.[84]

For purposes of the study, UP measured rates in terms of revenue per ton-mile, using its internal revenue accounting database for the complete census of traffic. Revenue per ton-mile figures were adjusted for inflation and discounts. The study, however, does not attempt to control for any other factors that may have caused revenue per ton-mile to change over time (e.g., productivity gains, changes in traffic mix, shipment characteristics, or input prices), so any conclusions about the direction and magnitude of rate changes should be viewed as tentative in nature.

-----

[82]The pre-merger period used as the benchmark for rate comparison purposes was October 1995 - March 1996. For the 2001 oversight hearings, for example, rates for October 2000 - March 2001 were compared to rates for October 1995 - March 1996.

[83]See STB-2001, at 3-4. According to STB-2000, the Board had previously offered to make UP's traffic tapes available under seal to interested parties to verify or rebut the reported downward trend in rates. Although the rate study was available to outside counsel and consultants to parties to the proceedings, according to Covington & Burling attorneys, the study was not challenged during the oversight proceedings.

[84]UP/SP-384, at Appendix E-1.

STB staff also conducted a rate study[85] – one that examines rate trends for rail traffic in the U.S. for the period 1984-99, using rates (revenue per ton-mile) for 15 commodity groups (farm products, coal, chemicals, lumber and wood, etc.), and separating rates for shipments originating in the West from those for shipments originating in the East. Data for the study come from the STB's non-public Carload Waybill Sample. The data show that inflation-adjusted U.S. rail rates have fallen 45.3% since 1984 (48.8% lower in the West and 40.7% lower in the East).[86] The STB attributes declining rates to productivity gains made in the aftermath of the 1980 Staggers Rail Act reforms that have been passed on to shippers. The study does not report rates for less aggregated commodity groups or for individual traffic lanes. It acknowledges that while average rail rates have fallen, not all rail customers have benefitted equally. Certain individual rates have increased and not all sectors have enjoyed the same level of rate declines.

The STB points to one chart showing that western rates were stable from 1992 to 1994, then resumed their decline once the restructuring of the western rail network began. If one uses the STB data to focus on the consummation of the UP/SP merger in 1996, we see, as the STB points out, that inflation-adjusted revenue per ton-mile in the West declined 9.2% (as compared to a decline of 5.1% in the East). Rail rates declined in the West during this period for 13 of the 15 commodity groups tracked, suggesting that rail mergers were responsible for the decline. The STB study, however, has limitations in addition to not focusing on less aggregated commodity groups or individual traffic lanes. It does not attempt to explain, using econometric methods, the level of rail rates over time, nor does it attempt to isolate the impact of the UP/SP merger on rail rates from other factors.[87]

GAO undertook a study to examine the effects of the 1996 UP/SP merger on rail rates,

---

[85]Surface Transportation Board, Office of Economics, Environmental Analysis, and Administration, *Rail Rates Continue Multi-Year Decline* (December 2000).

[86]The STB used a Tornqvist Index in its calculations to correct for any changes in traffic mix, particularly any shift toward low revenue per ton-mile traffic. A revenue per ton measure of rates was also calculated and produced similar results to that using revenue per ton-mile, suggesting that any tendency toward longer hauls was not driving the results.

[87]Another rail rate-trends study, with similar results, was conducted more recently by GAO. See General Accounting Office, *Railroad Regulation: Changes in Freight Railroad Rates from 1997 through 2000*. GAO-02-524 (June 2002). It too is based on the Carload Waybill Sample and uses revenue per ton-mile to measure rates. As compared to the STB study, GAO focused on more traffic corridors but fewer, more aggregated, commodity groups. The study finds that rail rates generally declined nationwide and for many of the commodities and traffic corridors examined. Rail rates for some commodities and distances, however, remained stable or increased. The study did not compare rail rates in the West with those in the East, as the STB had done. GAO identified factors that could explain observed rate changes for specific commodities and corridors (including the presence or absence of rail-to-rail or intermodal competition) but cautioned that its explanations were not meant to be definitive. GAO did not attempt to link rate changes to the UP/SP merger in this study.

apparently in response to concerns raised about the state of competition in the Central Corridor. GAO used a reduced form price (revenue per ton-mile) equation and a dummy variable to capture the impact of the merger.[88] The pre-merger period was 1994-95 and the post-merger period was 1997-99. GAO focused on two geographic areas (Reno and Salt Lake City), both in the Central Corridor and both having high concentrations of potential 2-to-1 shippers. These two areas provided relatively clear examples of cases where BNSF service substituted for SP service. The commodities considered were chemicals, coal, farm products, and non-metallic minerals. Six traffic movements were considered, e.g., chemicals to the Reno area, coal from the Salt Lake City area. The other explanatory variables include cost and demand factors, a dummy for the period of service disruption and delay, a dummy for whether a rail car is railroad-owned (as opposed to shipper-owned), and a dummy for whether the rate reflects a contract rate. In addition, a dummy variable was included to capture the effect of BNSF's presence as a competitor where otherwise the merger would have created 2-to-1 shippers.[89] Other factors, such as possible changes in the quality of service (aside from the service disruption period), were not incorporated. Nor did the data used to estimate the econometric model include a group of non-merging railroads (admittedly few in number in the West) to control for other changes during the time period under consideration.

GAO found that the merger by itself reduced rates for four (including coal) of the six commodity movements studied. For one commodity movement, post-merger rates were relatively unchanged (i.e., the change was not statistically significant), while the remaining commodity movement (chemicals to the Reno area) experienced a merger-related rate increase. In GAO's words, the "UP/SP merger generally decreased rail rates, but not for all commodities and not for all shippers." The coefficient for the dummy variable included to capture the extent of rail competition, i.e., BN/SF's presence, was negative (indicating reduced rates) and statistically significant for one traffic movement, while rates were essentially unchanged for the other three movements.[90] GAO did not reach any conclusion about the merits of the UP/SP merger. It did recommend that econometric techniques be used in future STB oversight proceedings to better isolate the impact of mergers on rates.

UP reportedly identified some shortcomings to GAO's empirical work but decided not to comment publicly. In a briefing for the author, Covington & Burling attorneys noted that some of the traffic examined was not representative. For example, the commodity movement for which rates increased involved a change in the composition of traffic from a lower-valued to a higher-valued chemical, the latter for which demand had increased. Also, according to outside counsel for UP, the GAO study did not withstand robustness tests UP staff performed on the

---

[88]See General Accounting Office, *Freight Railroad Regulation: Surface Transportation Board's Oversight Could Benefit From Evidence Better Identifying How Mergers Affect Rates.* GAO-01-689 (July 2001).

[89]Data were from the STB Carload Waybill Sample and the regression model was estimated using the SAS SURVEYREG procedure because the data are from stratified samples.

[90]Coal was excluded from this aspect of the analysis because of the absence of potential 2-to-1 shippers in the Salt Lake City and Reno areas.

estimation, i.e., it gave unexpected results when applied to other traffic.

A modified version of the GAO study was subsequently published in the Journal of Regulatory Economics.[91] The data sources and method are basically the same, as is the model to be estimated econometrically, but the traffic movements tested differed and the authors chose to highlight the rate impact of the trackage rights granted to BN/SF as a merger remedy. This version of the study excludes traffic movements involving Reno, and focuses on much higher volume movements of coal, chemicals, primary metals, farm products, petroleum, and food into or out of Salt Lake City (a total of eight traffic movements). The authors found that the merger by itself reduced rates for three commodities shipped from the area, and one commodity shipped to the area, remained essentially unchanged for three other movements, and increased for just one (chemicals to Salt Lake City). In addition, the coefficient for the dummy variable included to capture the competitive effect of BN/SF's presence was generally negative, indicating reduced rates. The latter finding is consistent with BN/SF being a more effective competitor post-merger than SP was pre-merger. The authors conclude that the trackage rights remedy for potential 2-to-1 shippers was effective.

In addition to rate studies directly related to STB's oversight hearings, Park et al. have used simulation methods to estimate the competitive effects of the BN/SF (Burlington Northern merged with Santa Fe in 1995) and UP/SP mergers on grain shipments from various subregions of Kansas to Houston, for export.[92] The researchers make use of a transportation cost-minimizing algorithm to derive least-cost wheat movements (based on data from the ICC Rail Costing Program) and a profit improvement algorithm to evaluate each railroad's ability to raise rates (Nash equilibrium prices) above variable costs. Oligopoly interaction is assumed to be characterized by price-setting behavior in a homogeneous goods industry. Mergers are simulated by dropping the restriction that railroads cannot interchange traffic and by eliminating interchange charges between merging railroads. The result, in some instances, is that the merger leads to a more direct routing of traffic, which is cost reducing. The simulations also assume the combined railroad adopts the cost structure of the lower cost merger partner. The major finding of the study is that the mergers resulted in negligible changes in market power for shipments from Kansas origins. The STB's measure of market power – the ratio of revenue to variable cost – was used for that purpose.[93] The authors conclude that a railroad's ability to raise rates is restricted if shippers can turn to at least one other railroad for freight service.

---

[91]John A. Karikari, Stephen M. Brown, and Mehrzad Hadji, "The Union Pacific/Southern Pacific Railroads Merger: Effect of Trackage Rights on Rates," *Journal of Regulatory Economics* 22 (2002), 271-285.

[92]Joon Je Park, Michael W. Babcock, Kenneth Lemke, and Dennis L. Weisman, "Simulating the Effects of Railroad Mergers," *Southern Economic Journal* 67 (2001), 938-953.

[93]UP's revenue to variable cost ratios declined marginally for shipments from two Kansas subregions while they increased 8.4% and 1.9% for shipments from the other two Kansas subregions. UP's (and BNSF's) resulting revenue to variable cost ratios for all four subregions were considered quite modest – at most 1.1 – relative to the fixed costs that also need to be covered.

In conclusion, the rate reduction data submitted by UP during the course of the oversight proceedings, and the rate study conducted by STB staff were generally consistent with the UP/SP merger having a pro-competitive effect and meeting even a consumer welfare standard. Neither the GAO study nor the paper by Park et al., each of which is narrowly focused on certain traffic segments, undercuts those findings. The UP and STB studies are not definitive, however, because they do not isolate the impact of the merger from other factors, including productivity gains, that could explain rate reductions. Nor was the STB staff study performed at a disaggregated level with respect to commodities and traffic corridors. With those caveats in mind, the UP rate study and STB staff study showing rate declines post-merger are also consistent with merger cost savings and efficiencies being realized and passed on to shippers in the form of lower rates.

G. Conclusions on Evidence of Realized Merger Benefits

Implementation of the merger plan in 1997 and 1998 was overshadowed by the service problems that affected UP/SP system-wide. Despite the prevailing conventional wisdom, the service problems were caused by a number of factors – not just management mistakes in implementing the merger – and the serious problems were overcome by the fall of 1998. STB oversight hearings, particularly toward the end of the five-year implementation period, suggest that substantial merger efficiencies (public benefits) were being achieved, but this is a preliminary finding based on the public record of the hearings.

Additional documentation of the realization of quantified benefits is provided by UP's internal tracking of merger efficiencies achieved. That shows ongoing benefits increasing during the merger implementation period, being realized in the areas contemplated by the operating plan, and exceeding projected amounts. Recent academic research also suggests that rail mergers, including UP/SP, have produced efficiency gains, although the study result for UP/SP should be viewed as tentative. Further confirmation of UP/SP merger efficiencies would have been provided by evidence of a declining operating ratio, as predicted in the merger application, but other factors – particularly the service problems of 1997-98 – obscured this relationship. Rail merger benefits were expected to translate into expanded single-line service and improved routings, and UP's confidential submission for the 2001 oversight hearings provided numerous examples of that happening. UP also made representations to securities analysts that it was realizing service improvements in these forms. Another development consistent with the achievement of substantial merger efficiencies was that planned capital expenditures, which were a prerequisite for obtaining cost savings and efficiencies, were undertaken, albeit in a form somewhat modified from that in the operating plan.

Indirect evidence that significant merger efficiencies were achieved would include customer satisfaction surveys showing improvement by the combined railroad, and rate reductions, post-merger. Shipper survey results, however, were mixed and not particularly reliable or informative. Available rate evidence from public and non-public sources, while not definitive, was generally consistent with merger cost savings and efficiencies being realized and being passed on to shippers in the form of lower rates.

Thus, available evidence indicates that UP has documented the realization of substantial merger efficiencies of the types claimed. Many of these were public in nature and merger-specific, i.e., attributable to the merger (not just to industry-wide productivity gains), and not reasonably achieved at that time through means short of merger. Admittedly, much of the evidence on realized merger efficiencies comes from UP itself and it was not closely scrutinized by the STB during its oversight hearings. Nonetheless, there are reasons for treating these claims as plausible. First, the realization of quantified benefits was tracked in considerable detail for management purposes, which made them verifiable and subject to challenge by those in UP management with the incentive to obtain accurate and unbiased information. Second, the nature of unquantified benefits realized is what would be expected from a merger with largely parallel, but also end-to-end elements, and their detailed enumeration makes them verifiable. Third, available evidence on rate reductions in the post-merger period is consistent with the realization of merger efficiencies that are passed on to shippers.

Although lessons from a single case study of a consummated railroad merger are limited, they do suggest that skepticism about merger-related efficiency claims may be overdone. Skepticism may be particularly inappropriate in a context where redundancies between merging parties seem prevalent, alternatives to merger appear limited, the parties have identified and documented efficiencies beforehand as part of a merger planning process, and they have a record of tracking efficiencies as part of a merger implementation plan. In these circumstances, the odds should improve that some efficiency claims meet regulatory standards and perhaps antitrust standards, i.e., are merger-specific, verifiable, and likely to be realized.

Bibliography

Berndt, Ernst R., Ann F. Friedlaender, Judy Shaw-Er Wang Chang, and Christopher A. Vellturo. "Cost Effects of Mergers and Deregulation in the U.S. Rail Industry." *The Journal of Productivity Analysis* 4 (1993) : 127-144.

Boyle, Matthew. *Fortune*. "America's Most Admired Companies." March 4, 2002.

Chapin, Allison, and Stephen Schmidt. "Do Mergers Improve Efficiency? Evidence from Deregulated Rail Freight." *Journal of Transport Economics and Policy* 33 (1999) : 147-162.

Christensen, Dr. Laurits R. Verified statement on behalf of the U.S. Department of Justice in DOJ-8 (April 9, 1996), redacted version. In *Union Pacific Corp. - Control & Merger - Southern Pacific Corp.*, STB Finance Docket 32760.

Conant, Michael. *Railroad Bankruptcies and Mergers from Chicago West: 1975-2001: Financial Analysis and Regulatory Critique. Research in Transportation Economics*, Vol. 7 (Amsterdam: Elsevier JAI, 2004).

Conrath, Craig W., and Nicholas A. Widnell. "Efficiency Claims in Merger Analysis: Hostility or Humility?" *George Mason Law Review* 7 (1999) : 685-705.

Draper, Mark J., and Dale W. Salzman. Verified statement on behalf of Union Pacific Corporation and Southern Pacific Corporation in UP/SP-22, "Railroad Merger Application" (November 30, 1995), Vol. 1, 361-370. In *Union Pacific Corp. - Control & Merger - Southern Pacific Corp.*, STB Finance Docket 32760.

Ellig, Jerry. "Railroad Deregulation and Consumer Welfare." *Journal of Regulatory Economics* 21 (2002): 143-167.

Evans, Ike, Union Pacific President and COO. "Strategy Recap." Presentation to Securities Analysts, New York City (November 28-29, 2001).

Grimm, Curtis M., and Joseph J. Plaistow. "Competitive Effects of Railroad Mergers." *Transportation Research Forum* 38 (1999) : 65-78.

Kaplan, Peter. *Washington Times*. "Grappling with Gridlock." December 3, 1997, p. B7.

Karikari, John A., Stephen M. Brown, and Mehrzad Hadji. "The Union Pacific/Southern Pacific Railroads Merger: Effect of Trackage Rights on Rates." *Journal of Regulatory Economics* 22 (2002) : 271-285.

King, Brad, Union Pacific Executive Vice President. "Network Optimization." Presentation to Securities Analysts, New York City (November 28-29, 2001).

Kwoka, Jr., John E., and Lawrence J. White. "Manifest Destiny? The Union Pacific and Southern Pacific Railroad Merger (1996)." In *The Antitrust Revolution: Economics, Competition, and Policy*, edited by John E. Kwoka, Jr. and Lawrence J. White, 27-51. New York: Oxford University Press, 2004.

McFarland, Henry B. "The Union Pacific–Southern Pacific Merger: What Can Be Learned?" *The Transportation Antitrust Update* (Spring 1999) : 5-10.

Machalaba, Daniel. *Wall Street Journal*. "Railroads Are Entering Alliances in Effort to Increase Efficiency." May 24, 2001.

Massa, Salvatore. "Are All Railroad Mergers in the Public Interest? An Analysis of the Union Pacific Merger with Southern Pacific." *Transportation Law Journal* 24 (Spring-Summer 1997) : 413-442.

National Industrial Traffic League, "Results of December 1999 Rail Merger Survey," in Statement of National Industrial Traffic League Before the Surface Transportation Board. In *Public Views on Major Rail Consolidations*, STB Ex Parte No. 582 (February 29, 2000).

Park, Joon Je, Michael W. Babcock, Kenneth Lemke, and Dennis L. Weisman. "Simulating the Effects of Railroad Mergers." *Southern Economic Journal* 67 (2001) : 938-953.

Pittman, Russell. "Railroads and Competition: The Santa Fe/Southern Pacific Merger Proposal." *Journal of Industrial Economics* 39 (September 1990) : 25-45.

Pittman, Russell. "Train Wreck: A Lesson in Megamergers," manuscript, June 1, 1998.

Sun, Huey-Lian, and Alex P. Tang. "The Sources of Railroad Merger Gains: Evidence from Stock Price Reaction and Operating Performance." *Transportation Journal* 39 (Summer 2000) : 14-26.

Surface Transportation Board. "General Oversight," Decision No. 13. In *Union Pacific Corp.–Control & Merger–Southern Pacific Corp.*, STB Finance Docket 32760 (Sub-No. 21). Decision served December 21, 1998.

_____. "General Oversight," Decision No. 15. In *Union Pacific Corp.–Control & Merger–Southern Pacific Corp.*, STB Finance Docket 32760 (Sub-No. 21). Decision served November 30, 1999.

_____. "General Oversight," Decision No. 16. In *Union Pacific Corp.–Control & Merger–Southern Pacific Corp.*, STB Finance Docket 32760 (Sub-No. 21). Decision served December 15, 2000.

_____. "General Oversight," Decision No. 21. In *Union Pacific Corp.–Control & Merger–Southern Pacific Corp.*, STB Finance Docket 32760 (Sub-No. 21). Decision served December 20, 2001.

_____. "Houston/Gulf Coast Oversight," Decision No. 10. In *Union Pacific Corp.–Control & Merger–Southern Pacific Corp.*, STB Finance Docket 32760 (Sub-No. 26). Decision served December 21, 1998.

_____. "Joint Petition for Further Service Order," STB Service Order No. 1518. Decision served February 17, 1998.

_____. "Joint Petition for Further Service Order," STB Service Order No. 1518 (Sub-No. 1). Decision served July 31, 1998.5

_____. *Major Rail Consolidation Procedures,* STB Ex Parte No. 582 (Sub-No. 1). Decision served June 11, 2001.

_____. "Oversight," Decision No. 10. In *Union Pacific Corp.–Control & Merger–Southern Pacific Corp.*, STB Finance Docket 32760 (Sub-No. 21). Decision served October 27, 1997.

_____. *Union Pacific/Southern Pacific Merger*, 1 S.T.B. 233 (1996).

Surface Transportation Board, Office of Economics, Environmental Analysis, and Administration. *Rail Rates Continue Multi-Year Decline*. December 2000.

Valentine, James J. "Freight Pulse Survey: Second Round Insights." *Equity Research: Freight Transportation*. Morgan Stanley, January 11, 2002.

White, Lawrence J. "Staples-Office Depot and UP-SP: An Antitrust Tale of Two Proposed Mergers." In *Measuring Market Power*, edited by Daniel J. Slottje, 153-174. *Contributions to Economic Analysis*, Vol. 255 (Amsterdam: Elsevier Science, North-Holland, 2002).

Wilson, Wesley, and John Bitzan. "Industry Costs and Consolidation: Efficiency Gains and Mergers in the Railroad Industry." Upper Great Plains Transportation Institute, MPC Report No. 03-145 (June 2003).

Yarberry, Lawrence C. Verified statement on behalf of Union Pacific Corporation and Southern Pacific Corporation in UP/SP-22, "Railroad Merger Application" (November 30, 1995), Vol. 1, 251-289. In *Union Pacific Corp. - Control & Merger - Southern Pacific Corp.*, STB Finance Docket 32760.

Union Pacific Corporation. *2001 Annual Report*.

_____. Comments of Union Pacific Corporation and Union Pacific Railroad Company Before the Surface Transportation Board. In *Public Views of Major Rail Consolidations*, STB Ex Parte No. 582 (February 29, 2000).

_____. UP/SP-384, "Union Pacific's Fifth Annual Oversight Report" (July 2, 2001), confidential version. In *Union Pacific Corp. - Control & Merger - Southern Pacific Corp.*, STB Finance Docket 32760.

_____. UP/SP-384, "Union Pacific's Fifth Annual Oversight Report" (July 2, 2001), public version. In *Union Pacific Corp. - Control & Merger - Southern Pacific Corp.*, STB Finance Docket 32760.

Union Pacific Corporation and Southern Pacific Corporation. UP/SP-22, "Railroad Merger Application" (November 30, 1995), Vol. 1. In *Union Pacific Corp. - Control & Merger - Southern Pacific Corp.*, STB Finance Docket 32760.

_____. UP/SP-24, "Railroad Merger Application" (November 30, 1995), Vol. 3. In *Union Pacific Corp. - Control & Merger -Southern Pacific Corp.*, STB Finance Docket 32760.

Union Pacific Railroad Company. "Annual Report to the Securities and Exchange Commission." Form 10-K for fiscal year ended December 31, 1997.

_____. "Annual Report to the Securities and Exchange Commission." Form 10-K for fiscal year ending December 31, 1999.

_____. "Closing the Gap: Customer Satisfaction (1998-2000)." Undated company document.

_____. "Merger Benefits and Costs: Ongoing Merger Benefits." Undated company document.

_____. "Quarterly Report to the Securities and Exchange Commission." Form 10-Q for the quarter ending June 30, 1998.

U.S. Department of Justice. Brief Before the Surface Transportation Board (June 3, 1996), redacted version. DOJ-14 in *Union Pacific Corp. – Control & Merger – Southern Pacific Corp.*, STB Finance Docket 32760.

U.S. Department of Justice and Federal Trade Commission. *Horizontal Merger Guidelines.* (1992, rev'd 1997).

U.S. General Accounting Office. *Freight Railroad Regulation: Surface Transportation Board's Oversight Could Benefit From Evidence Better Identifying How Mergers Affect Rates.* GAO-01-689 (July 2001).

_____. *Railroad Regulation: Changes in Freight Railroad Rates from 1997 through 2000.* GAO-02-524 (June 2002).